The Blood
Study Guide

The Blood Study Guide

Benny Hinn

Charisma®
HOUSE
Books about Spirit-Led Living

THE BLOOD STUDY GUIDE by Benny Hinn
Published by Charisma House
A part of Strang Communications Company
600 Rinehart Road
Lake Mary, FL 32746
www.charismahouse.com

Unless otherwise noted, all Scripture quotations are
from the New King James Version of the Bible.
Copyright © 1979, 1980, 1982 by Thomas Nelson, Inc.,
publishers. Used by permission.

Scripture quotations marked KJV are from the
King James Version of the Bible.

Scripture quotations marked NIV are from the Holy Bible,
New International Version. Copyright © 1973, 1978, 1984,
International Bible Society. Used by permission.

Library of Congress Catalog Card Number: 95-83821
International Standard Book Number: 0-88419-428-0

01 02 03 04 05   7 6 5 4 3 2 1
Printed in the United States of America

TABLE OF CONTENTS

Week Five
There's New Life in the Blood

Week Six
Jesus, Our Mediator: Grace in His Blood

Week Seven
God's Grace and Your New Family

Week Eight
Communion in the Communion

The Leader's Guide

INTRODUCTION

There is power in the blood of Jesus. There is no question about it. But at the same time, the blood does not have "magical" power. The power comes from Jesus and His finished work on the cross. He is the One who will act on your behalf when you apply His blood through prayer.

We apply Jesus' blood through prayer and faith. But it is the Lord who covers us; we do not cover ourselves.

Why have I written this study guide on the blood?

- To open your eyes to the importance God places on the topic of the blood covenant

- To demonstrate the power of the blood of Jesus

- To show how you and I can come into God's presence through the blood of His Son

- To help you understand the "great" grace that God bestows on us because of the blood of Jesus

- To point you to a greater freedom in Christ than you have ever experienced

- To help you explore the Word and discover the mighty power of the blood of Jesus

- To equip you to apply the blood in your own spiritual life

- To enable you to evaluate, examine and explore your relationship with Jesus Christ through the awesome power of His blood

You will want to read and complete this study with your Bible open. God places great emphasis on the blood from Genesis to Revelation. Therefore, there is a message in His Word for you.

As you go through this study:

- Keep your Bible open, ready to read every passage.

- Complete each exercise and write every prayer suggested.

- Be open and honest with the Lord and with yourself.

- Share what you learn about the blood with others.

- Memorize the suggested Scripture verses at the beginning of each week.

This study is for:

- Individual believers studying about the blood

- Small discipleship groups or home groups

- Prayer and Bible study groups

- Sunday school classes

- Men's and women's groups

The Leader's Guide at the back of this study manual will help group leaders, teachers and facilitators to guide a group of people through an in-depth study of the blood of Jesus Christ.

If you have picked up this study of the blood and have not read my book *The Blood,* I encourage you to read the book and use it as a part of your group study.

When I asked the Holy Spirit to give me an understanding of the blood covenant, I had many questions, including:

- What does the Scripture in Hebrews 12:24 mean when it says the blood "speaks better things than that of Abel"?

- How can the blood of Jesus be applied in our lives today?

- How is God's grace connected to the blood of His Son?

- How can the blood of Christ provide protection for my household?

- What does Scripture teach about the blood of the cross and the anointing of the Holy Spirit?

- How can we use the blood of Jesus to defeat the enemy in our lives?

God gave me answers from His Word, and I want to share them with you. I pray that you will experience God's wonderful presence as you continue reading and studying about the blood covenant and learning to understand its effectiveness in your own life.

POWER AND PROMISE
IN THE BLOOD

Israel is a unique and wonderful land. For the first sixteen years of my life it was all I knew, for I was born in Jaffa, Israel.

Although the majority of Jaffa's citizens are Jewish, my family was not. My mother, Clemence, was of Armenian descent. And my father, Costandi, came from a family that had immigrated from Greece to Egypt and then to Palestine. To add to my multicultural childhood, I was christened in the Greek Orthodox church, spoke French at school, Arabic in our home and Hebrew outside the home.

Immediately after the long, terrifying days of war and conflict known as the Six-Day War of 1967, my father gathered our family of eight children together and announced that we would be emigrating to another country. The next year we arrived in Toronto, Canada, with just a few earthly possessions. At age sixteen, I suddenly found myself in a new country where the culture, climate and language were different. The changes meant a new school, new acquaintances and even new and different clothing, for I was suddenly forced to cope with cold and snow for months on end.

Initially, all of these changes were very traumatic for me. But in 1972 my life was totally transformed by an encounter with Christ at a morning prayer meeting conducted by students at the school I attended. At home after school that day, I opened the pages of a big black Bible that had not been used for years. After reading from the Gospels nonstop for several hours, I found myself saying aloud, "Jesus, come into my heart."

I thank God He did.

Later that same week I accompanied my newfound Christian friends to their church. The people who attended there were an exuberant throng of Christians who met every Thursday in St. Paul's Cathedral, an Anglican church located in downtown Toronto. I had never heard people speak so openly about the blood of Christ. They would sing, "Oh, the blood of Jesus!" They would pray, "Lord, cover us with Your blood." As you study about the blood this week, it is my prayer that the Lord Jesus would cover you with His blood.

THIS WEEK'S OVERVIEW

DAY	STUDY TOPIC
ONE	There's Power in the Blood
TWO	Chaos in the Garden
THREE	The Flesh and the Devil
FOUR	Temptation and the Throne of God
FIVE	Putting on the Armor of God

Each day be sure to:

1. Read the study materials thoroughly.
2. Read every Scripture passage. (Use several different Bible translations to study the passages you are not able to understand easily.)
3. Answer each study question and complete each exercise with total honesty and openness.
4. Pray for wisdom, understanding and insight.
5. Apply what you learn about the blood to your daily walk in the Spirit.

I am excited for you as you begin this first week of study. Each week you will:

- Discover that the blood of Jesus has power and promise for your life.

- Better understand God's plan for your life.

- Comprehend the chaos caused by the sin of Adam and Eve in the Garden of Eden.

- Examine the areas of sin where your own flesh is tempted.

- Begin to use the Word of God as a mighty weapon against the enemy, satan.

Memory Verse

This week, memorize Romans 5:9:"Much more then, having now been justified by His [Jesus'] blood, we shall be saved from wrath through Him [Jesus]."

I know that the Holy Spirit is going to do a marvelous work in your life as you study about the blood in His Word. This is my prayer for you this week:

Lord Jesus, I pray that in the coming week You will cover this person with Your precious blood. Fill him (or her) to overflowing with Your precious Holy Spirit that he (or she) might know the power of Your blood. In Jesus' mighty name, amen.

THERE'S POWER
IN THE BLOOD

Our home in Jaffa, Israel, seemed much larger than it was. To save land the building we lived in was designed for three families, with a separate home on each level. On the top floor lived Mr. Hanna and his family. He was Lebanese, married to a Jewish woman from Hungary. But Mr. Hanna was more than a neighbor. Because of the bond that was established between my father and him, he became almost a second father to the eight children in our family. As a result of their relationship, Mr. Hanna and my father made a commitment to one another in a very dramatic way.

Mr. Hanna and my father, Costandi, entered into a pact that will never be erased from my memory. Using a razor-sharp blade, each man made an incision on his wrist until blood seeped to the surface. Then they placed their wrists tightly together and allowed the blood to mingle.

On the table before them were two glasses of wine. My father held his wrist over one of the goblets and let several drops of blood fall into it. Mr. Hanna did the same with the second glass.

Next, they mixed the wine together, and each drank from the other man's cup. At that moment they became blood brothers. In the Eastern culture and among many other people of the world, it is the strongest bond that can be made between two men.

It is more than a legal pact. It is a vow that is sealed in blood and will never be broken. This practice dates back thousands of years in the Middle East. It's called the blood covenant.

When our family emigrated from Israel to Canada and I became a Christian, the Holy Spirit began to reveal God's Word to me. I had seen the influence of the blood pact in the Eastern culture. Then the Holy Spirit showed me how much more powerful God's blood covenant is. From Genesis to Revelation there is a crimson stream—the life-giving source of power, protection and promise for you and for me today.

The shedding of blood, even today, refers to giving life. Check (✔) all the things you think of when "shedding blood" is mentioned. Use the blank line to add any other thoughts:

❏ Someone dying for his or her country during wartime

❏ A martyr dying for a cause or belief

❏ A friend donating blood

❏ An organ donor dying and giving organs for others to live

❏ Any sacrifice of life or injury given for a just cause

❏ _____

In Old Testament times, animals were sacrificed as part of the blood covenant that God established with His people. Throughout history the blood covenant has been used in the natural as an expression of brotherhood or commitment between two individuals. It also served as a temporary means of atonement for sin under the Old Covenant.

We can learn many spiritual lessons from a study of the blood. Although the blood covenant has even greater significance in the spirit realm, let's begin with a look at the first blood sacrifice recorded in Scripture. Read Genesis 3:21.

The First Blood Sacrifice

> Also for Adam and his wife the LORD God made tunics of skin, and clothed them.
>
> —GENESIS 3:21

Who made the decision to shed blood? Describe (✍) whose blood was shed and why:

_____

_____

_____

_____

_____

In the following words from Paul, **underline** the phrase that means the most to you:

> You see, at just the right time, when we were still powerless, Christ died for the ungodly. Very rarely will anyone die for a righteous man, though for a good man someone might possibly dare to die. But God demonstrates his own love for us in this: While we were still sinners, Christ died for us. Since we have now been justified by his blood, how much more shall we be saved from God's wrath through him!
>
> —ROMANS 5:6-9, NIV

Now, pray this prayer aloud:

> *Lord Jesus, I thank You for the blood covenant. I praise You for shedding Your blood for me before I ever knew You! Thank You, wonderful Lord Jesus, a million thanks.*

CHAOS IN THE GARDEN

In order to comprehend the tremendous power of the blood covenant, it is important to recall what happened in the Garden of Eden. When God created Adam, he was a perfect being. He had a mind so magnificent that he was able to name every animal and remember their names.

At that time, the first man and woman lived in perfect harmony with God. He walked with them in the cool of the day. They had fellowship with God and knew Him intimately.

But an enemy was lurking in the garden.

> Now the serpent was more cunning than any beast of the field which the LORD God had made. And he said to the woman, "Has God indeed said, 'You shall not eat of every tree of the garden'?"
>
> —GENESIS 3:1

Satan was cunning and sly. He came to the woman with a question about God's instructions regarding eating from the tree.

The devil wields this weapon of words because he wants us to question God's faithfulness, love, promises and power. He was asking the woman: "Did God really say that?" Her answer shows she believed the tempter rather than what God said because she disobeyed.

The woman replied to the serpent, "We may eat the fruit of the trees of the garden; but of the fruit of the tree which is in the midst of the garden, God has said, 'You shall not eat it, nor shall you touch it, *lest you die*'" (Gen. 3:2-3, emphasis added).

Look closely at what the woman said. **Read** Genesis 2:16-17. Now read carefully what the woman said that God said. How did Eve change what God had said? **Describe** (✐) her change:

_____

_____

_____

Then satan lied to the woman and said, "You will not surely die. For God knows that in the day you eat of it your eyes will be opened, and you will be like God, knowing good and evil" (Gen. 3:4-5).

Satan had been banished from heaven for trying to be like God. Yet now he was attempting to offer godlike status to the first woman. And he has not stopped. Thousands of years later, he is still planting the same thoughts into unsuspecting hearts.

Are you worshiping the *God who is,* or do you find yourself trying to have it your own way? On the lines below, **describe** (✍) a time when you may have tried to get God to do things your own way. What were the results of your attempt?

_____

_____

_____

_____

_____

_____

_____

_____

_____

Adam and Eve created chaos in their lives by disobeying God. They refused to acknowledge His complete sovereignty over their lives. They tried to *play* God instead of *obeying* God. Satan tempts us to disobey God's ways and to do things our way. **Read** Exodus 20:1-17. These are the Ten Commandments given to Moses on Mount Sinai. This is a good point in this study for you to consider and examine your obedience to God.

It is impossible to obey God without the power of the precious Holy Spirit. It is impossible to obey God until we are fully surrendered to Jesus Christ as our Lord and Savior. If you have accepted Jesus Christ as your personal Lord and Savior, pray the following prayer as a rededication to trusting and obeying Him. If you have not accepted Jesus, pray to receive Jesus right now:

Wonderful Lord, You alone are the Messiah, the Son of the living God. I ask You to forgive and cleanse me of all my sins through Your shed blood. I surrender to You, wonderful Jesus, as my Lord and Savior. Fill me with Your precious Holy Spirit that I might have Your power to trust and obey You with all my heart. Thank You, in the mighty name of Jesus. Amen.

THE FLESH
AND THE DEVIL

The first woman not only fell for the lie, but her husband, Adam, did, too. And sin entered the heart of mankind. "So when the woman saw that the tree was good for food, that it was pleasant to the eyes, and a tree desirable to make one wise, she took its fruit and ate. She also gave to her husband with her, and he ate" (Gen. 3:6).

In that one Scripture verse we find three great temptations satan uses:

- The lust of the flesh (The tree was good for food.)

- The lust of the eyes (It was pleasant to look at.)

- The pride of life (The tree offered wisdom.)

Today, believers can know how to resist the three temptations to which Adam and Eve succumbed. We can resist—not because we are any stronger or better than they were—but because we can use the mighty power of the Holy Spirit to resist temptation. How does this power work to help us resist? **Read** each of the following verses and **describe** (✍) what God's Word reveals about the power of the Holy Spirit within us to resist the devil.

God's Word	The power to resist satan is . . .
Zechariah 4:6	_____
Acts 2:38	_____
Ephesians 1:19–23	_____
1 John 3:8; 4:4	_____

Satan was defeated at the cross of Jesus Christ by His shed blood. The only power the devil has is to harass, tempt and attack you. But he cannot succeed if you resist him.

Using the power of the Holy Spirit within you, you have the power to refuse temptation and to stand firm in Christ Jesus. **Read** 1 Peter 5:8-9, and then **describe** (✐) how to resist satan's attack.

_____

_____

In order to use the Word, as Christians we must first know it! Is the Word of God hidden in your heart? How important is the Word? Read what the Bible says. **Look up** each passage and **complete** the sentence:

- We must _____ God's Word in our hearts so that we will not _____ against God (Ps. 119:11).

- When the righteous person _____ on God's law day and night, that person will prosper (Ps. 1:2).

- God's Word is a _____ that pierces our soul and spirit and reveals the thoughts and intents of our hearts (Heb. 4:12).

- All Scripture is _____ for our doctrine, reproof, correction, and instruction (2 Tim. 3:16).

You can't use what you don't have or know. Ignorance of God's Word leads to failure, disobedience and an inability to resist temptation. How successfully have you been resisting the devil? The three major areas of temptation are listed below. Draw a **circle** (◯) around the answer that best describes your ability to resist.

1. **The lust of the flesh** (for example, overeating, being obsessed with personal appearance, being sexually impure)
    I **(never) (rarely) (sometimes) (usually) (always)** am able to resist the devil.

2. **The lust of the eyes** (for example, desiring what you may want but don't need, looking at another person with lust in your heart, letting your eyes rest more on the things of the world—TV, movies, entertainment— rather than the things of God—His Word, worship, loving and serving Him and others)

I (never) (rarely) (sometimes) (usually) (always) am able to resist the devil.

3. **The pride of life** (for example, being self-serving and arrogant, trusting in your own intellectual abilities, physical strength or talents rather than God, asking God to bless your plans instead of seeking His plan and will)
I (never) (rarely) (sometimes) (usually) (always) am able to resist the devil.

If one of these areas of temptation is a problem in your life, then take the first step—*admit it and quit it*. Repent! Confess it to the Lord and ask for His forgiveness.

Make a determination to build your strength to resist temptation when satan confronts you with it. Listed below are some things that will help to strengthen you. Check **(✔)** the ones that you think will be helpful to you. Then determine in your heart to do these things.

❑ Spend more time reading and memorizing the Word.

❑ Set aside a time each day for Bible study and prayer.

❑ Become a part of a regular Bible study class or group.

❑ Find a spiritual mentor or Bible study partner who can teach you the Word and with whom you can be honest and accountable.

❑ Find a church or fellowship of believers that teaches and believes God's Word.

Start doing these things this week. Get the Word in you. Then you will be prepared to resist the attacks of the devil.

Pray a prayer of repentance for yielding to these three great temptations. As you repent, accept God's forgiveness (1 John 1:9). In faith thank the Lord for victory and the power to stop yielding to satan.

TEMPTATION AND
THE THRONE OF GOD

Yesterday we studied the three great areas of temptation facing the believer—the lust of the flesh, the lust of the eyes and the pride of life. Satan tried to tempt Jesus in these same three areas during his encounter with the Lord in the desert.

Satan presented his temptations to Jesus through his knowledge of the Word. But Jesus with the authority of heaven used the Word to defeat him. Jesus said, "You shall not tempt the LORD your God" (Matt. 4:7). Three separate times He said: "It is written" (Matt. 4:4, 7, 10). Finally, Jesus said, "Away with you, Satan! For it is written, 'You shall worship the LORD your God, and Him only you shall serve'" (Matt. 4:10).

Coming into God's presence involves the total sacrifice and surrender of ourselves before the Lord. **Circle** (◯) the words from Romans 12:1-2 below that speak most directly to you.

> I beseech you therefore, brethren, by the mercies of God, that you present your bodies a living sacrifice, holy, acceptable to God, which is your reasonable service. And do not be conformed to this world, but be transformed by the renewing of your mind, that you may prove what is that good and acceptable and perfect will of God.

In the Old Testament or covenant, worship was only possible through the blood sacrifice. The Hebrews would shed the blood of bulls, lambs and doves to provide a temporary covering of blood so that worship at the temple might be sanctified.

When Jesus shed His blood on the cross, He became the supreme sacrifice. The shed blood of Jesus gives you access to the throne of God any time, any place and in any circumstance. **Describe** (✍) what each of the following passages says about the presence of God through the shed blood of Christ.

Hebrews 9:11-15 _____

_____

_____

Hebrews 10:19-25 _____

_____

_____

How do you feel when you approach the throne of God? **Check** (✔) the attitudes below that represent your own feelings about the throne of God.

❑ Afraid   ❑ Guilty

❑ Bold   ❑ Ashamed

❑ Joyful   ❑ Thankful

❑ Condemned   ❑ In awe and wonder

❑ Other: _____

If you checked some negative, guilt-ridden feelings, stop and ask Jesus to cleanse you and cover you with His blood. As you do, the guilt of your past will fade away, and you can approach Him boldly as a forgiven, victorious saint—for so you are!

Satan wants no part of worshiping God. He rebelled from the presence and worship of God. So, as you worship, he flees. As you enter the throne room of the Father through the shed blood of Jesus, satan is powerless to touch, attack, harass or accuse you. Here are some practical steps that you can take to approach the Father's throne boldly through the blood.

• Praying boldly

• Praying in the Spirit

• Singing praises to the Lord and playing praise music

• Shouting unto God with the voice of triumph

• Applying the blood of Jesus to every person and circumstance

• Serving and ministering unto the Lord by serving others in His name

- Loving the Lord with all your heart, mind, soul and strength

- Surrendering to His will and way for your daily walk

- Giving Him glory and praise, taking no glory for yourself

Read the preceding list one more time. **Circle (◯)** the practical steps that you have used regularly to approach God's throne. On the following lines, **describe (✍)** how you could use the remaining steps in your personal life to build your faith and bring you closer to God's throne.

_____

_____

The devil is well aware of the power of the blood and wants nothing to do with it. If we are submitted, surrendered and following Jesus, then satan will not be found near us. When we get out from under the covering of His blood and rebel against the Lord, then we open ourselves up to the enemy's attack.

God's Word is a powerful weapon against the enemy's attacks because it reveals to us the conditions and promises of God's blood covenant. From the moment man sinned, God introduced the blood covenant as a means of covering or atonement. Start speaking, worshiping and exalting the Lord through the Word. Pray the Word.

> *Bless the LORD, O my soul,*
> *And forget not all His benefits:*
> *Who forgives all your iniquities,*
> *Who heals all your diseases,*
> *Who redeems your life from destruction,*
> *Who crowns you with lovingkindness and tender*
>   *mercies,*
> *Who satisfies your mouth with good things,*
> *So that your youth is renewed like the eagle's. Amen.*
>   —FROM PSALM 103:2–5

PUTTING ON THE
ARMOR OF GOD

I n Jesus Christ you have the authority to crush satan. Read Romans 16:20. In your own words, **describe** (✍) what it says:

_____

_____

_____

How do we crush satan under our feet and defeat his strategies? We do it by putting on the armor of God. This armor has been given to you by the Captain of the Hosts of God—Jesus Himself. Too often we fail to put on the whole armor of God as the Scripture declares and start our day with our own armor, which is inadequate and full of holes. Without His armor we set ourselves up for attack, harassment and pointless struggle.

Decide today to cover yourself with God's armor. The blood of Jesus makes it possible for you to have the full armor of God, which includes the "sword of the Spirit"—the Word of God.

The Bible tells us to put on God's armor. Notice that the armor of God is a covering, just as is the blood of Jesus Christ. It all fits together. We have no right to put on God's armor until we are first cleansed, purified and covered with the blood. The blood prepares us to receive the armor.

Look up the following verses and **describe** (✍) what each verse has to say about God's armor.

The Bible	The Armor of God
1 Thessalonians 5:8	_____
Isaiah 49:2	_____
Hebrews 4:12	_____

Read Ephesians 6:10-18. These verses tell us how to prepare and equip ourselves to be a "good soldier of Jesus Christ" (2 Tim. 2:3). Complete the following description of God's armor, indicating what each piece represents spiritually.

Piece of Armor	Spiritual Application
_____	_____
_____	_____
_____	_____
_____	_____
_____	_____
_____	_____

Consider the sword of the Spirit—the Word of God. Revelation 12:11 declares, "They [the saints] overcame him by the blood of the Lamb and by the word of their testimony." That is powerful! The blood and the Word work together to defeat the enemy. My testimony is not what *I* have done but what *Jesus*, as the Word, has done through His blood and manifested in my life through His Word.

Write (✍) your testimony of what Jesus, the Word of God, has done in your life by completing the following statements. Find a portion of Scripture to support your statements.

1. Jesus saved me when _____

    _____

    Scripture: _____

2. Jesus' blood washed me _____

    _____

    Scripture: _____

3. The Holy Spirit baptized me when _____

    _____

    Scripture: _____

4. The Spirit filled me as_____

    _____

    Scripture: _____

5. I praise Jesus for _____

    Scripture: _____

6. I have repented of and been forgiven for_____

    Scripture: _____

7. One miracle that God is doing in my life right now is___

    Scripture: _____

As the blood covers and cleanses you, Jesus makes you armed and dangerous through the mighty armor of God. You can withstand and defeat the wiles of the devil.

Pray the following prayer aloud, putting on God's armor and preparing for victory. Do this daily, putting on Jesus, putting on the blood, taking up the Sword of the Spirit and standing firm!

> *Lord Jesus, cleanse me and cover me with Your blood. I gird my loins with Your truth. I cover my heart with the breastplate of Your righteousness. I cover my feet, my walk in Your Spirit, with Your peace. I put on the helmet of Your salvation through Your shed blood. I take up the shield of faith, Your Word, with which I will defeat satan through Your Word and blood.*
>
> *In the name of the Mighty Warrior, Jesus. Amen.*

THE BLOOD'S COVERING
AND COVENANT

When Adam and his wife yielded to the snare of satan, "the eyes of both of them were opened, and they knew that they were naked; and they sewed fig leaves together and made themselves coverings" (Gen. 3:7). The fact that they even tried to make clothes for themselves showed that they realized their need for a covering.

The instant they yielded to temptation they lost their God-consciousness and gained self-consciousness. They lost sight of God and His glory.

I am fully convinced that before the Fall the first man and woman did not see their physical nakedness as shameful. They may have been without the clothing that you and I wear, but I believe they were covered with the glory of God. Psalm 8:5 declares, "You made him a little lower than the heavenly beings and crowned him with glory and honor" (NIV).

Because they were accustomed to being blanketed by God, after they sinned they made themselves a covering (Gen. 3:7). When they first gained sight of self, they realized how empty and exposed they truly were and even "hid themselves from the presence of the LORD God among the trees of the garden" (v. 8).

But God had a plan for a better covering. This week we will study God's intervention into Adam and Eve's life with a covering of blood. We will see how that event foreshadowed God's plan to cover us with the blood of His own Son, Christ Jesus. As we study, we will explore the beginnings of the blood covenant in the Bible.

Remember my father and Mr. Hanna? Thousands of people have entered into a blood covenant like the one my father and Mr. Hanna made. In the Old Testament it was common for men to "cut a covenant" and make a pact through the shedding of blood. (See Genesis 15:10; 21:27.)

Accounts of blood covenants are not only found in Scripture, but also in history. The shedding of blood in a covenant is still practiced in various parts of the world. We will learn how God established the foundation for an eternal blood covenant with us through Abraham in the Old Testament.

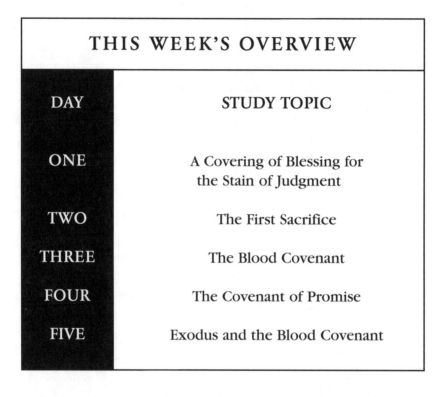

THIS WEEK'S OVERVIEW

DAY	STUDY TOPIC
ONE	A Covering of Blessing for the Stain of Judgment
TWO	The First Sacrifice
THREE	The Blood Covenant
FOUR	The Covenant of Promise
FIVE	Exodus and the Blood Covenant

During your study of the covering of the blood and the blood covenant this week, you will:

- Recognize the meaning of sacrifice in the Old Testament.

- Understand the atoning power of the blood.

- Learn how sin brings curses into our lives.

- Discover why God accepted Abel's sacrifice but did not accept Cain's sacrifice.

- See that the covenant of promise God made with Abraham became the foundation of God's eternal blood covenant with His people.

As you read, study, meditate on Scripture and apply God's truths in your own life this week, I pray that the wonderful covering of the blood of Jesus will become real in your life.

Memory Verse

I encourage you to memorize Exodus 24:6-7.

> And Moses took half the blood and put it in basins, and half the blood he sprinkled on the altar. Then he took the Book of the Covenant and read in the hearing of the people. And they said, "All that the LORD has said we will do, and be obedient."

A Covering of Blessing
for the Stain of Judgment

Wherever God is, the blessings of life exist. In His absence, there is death. As long as Adam and Eve stayed in His presence, they experienced the blessings of God. But when they disobeyed Him, leaving His presence, they experienced the curse of sin and death.

The blessing of God covered them with His glory. After they ate the fruit from the Tree of the Knowledge of Good and Evil, they separated themselves from God through sin and experienced existence without the covering of God's glory. Without the covering of His blessing, His presence and His blood, we face the judgments of God.

Because of their disobedience, judgment fell upon Adam and Eve. Because of their sin, God pronounced five separate judgments (Gen. 3:14-19). As we study these five judgments, we will discover that the same judgments fall upon us when we are physically born. That's right. As children of Adam and Eve, we are born under these judgments. They can only be removed by the covering of the blood of Jesus.

Below is the account of God's judgment following Adam and Eve's sin. **Read** the passage, **underlining** each judgment that you find in the passage. Then check your list against the one I will give you.

So the LORD God said to the serpent:

"Because you have done this,
You are cursed more than all cattle,
And more than every beast of the field;
On your belly you shall go,
And you shall eat dust
All the days of your life.
And I will put enmity
Between you and the woman,

And between your seed and her Seed;
He shall bruise your head,
And you shall bruise His heel."

To the woman He said:

"I will greatly multiply your sorrow and your
    conception;
In pain you shall bring forth children;
Your desire shall be for your husband,
And he shall rule over you."

Then to Adam He said, "Because you have heeded the
voice of your wife, and have eaten from the tree of
which I commanded you, saying, 'You shall not eat of it':

"Cursed is the ground for your sake;
In toil you shall eat of it
All the days of your life.
Both thorns and thistles it shall bring forth for you,
And you shall eat the herb of the field.
In the sweat of your face you shall eat bread
Till you return to the ground,
For out of it you were taken;
For dust you are,
And to dust you shall return."

—GENESIS 3:14-19

Compare your answers with God's judgments.

1. God cursed the serpent.
2. God pronounced judgment on Eve.
3. The Lord judged Adam to a life of toil.
4. God cursed the ground.
5. The Lord sentenced Adam to eventual death.

We are born under these judgments. We are born separated from
God, into a state of sin. The Bible declares, "Behold, I was shapen in
iniquity; and in sin did my mother conceive me" (Ps. 51:5, KJV).
Jeremiah 17:9 tells us, "The heart is deceitful above all things, and
desperately wicked; who can know it?"

From the time of Adam and Eve's disobedience in the Garden, mankind has struggled to become free of the judgment of God. Even God's standard of the law, given to Moses on Mount Sinai, was ineffectual to free man from the judgment of God. It was a standard that was impossible for man to keep because of his sinful state. (See Galatians 3:10-12.)

Yet, in spite of the state of sin into which we are born, there is hope. **Read** Genesis 3:15 and **describe** (✍) God's promise in your own words.

> And I will put enmity between you and the woman, and between your seed and her Seed; He shall bruise your head, and you shall bruise His heel.

Out of Eve's seed would come a man who would destroy satan's works and liberate us from the judgment of God. Of course, we know that man was the Messiah, Jesus Christ. Because of Adam and Eve's disobedience and the subsequent judgment of God, mankind could not hope to attain the righteousness required by God's law through our own efforts. It is only by the sacrificial shed blood of Christ that we have been redeemed. "He [Christ] redeemed us in order that the blessing given to Abraham might come to the Gentiles through Christ Jesus, so that by faith we might receive the promise of the Spirit" (Gal. 3:14, NIV). That is a victory in which every believer shares.

Write (✍) a prayer now, thanking God for breaking the judgment of God put upon us by the sin of Adam and Eve. Thank God for the Messiah who came to destroy satan's power. Give praise to God for the shed blood of Jesus.

THE FIRST SACRIFICE

Wh! Adam and Eve rebelled against God, God did something marvelous. He initiated the first blood sacrifice.

> Unto Adam also and to his wife did the LORD God make coats of skins, and clothed them.
>
> —GENESIS 3:21, KJV

Sin removed Adam and Eve from the presence of God: therefore they had lost His glory. They were naked and ashamed, attempting to cover themselves with leaves. That is when God selected some animals, perhaps lambs, and killed them. He covered the man and woman with skins of the slain animals (Gen. 3:21). I believe that the animals had just been slain and that the skins were still moist with blood when God used them to cover Adam and Eve.

Please note: God's first sacrifice covered Adam and Eve's sin with animals' blood. As we will see, His final sacrifice covered you and me with the blood of His only begotten Son. When the Bible says, "It is the blood that makes atonement for the soul" (Lev. 17:11), the word *atonement* means "to cover." That is why I believe the shedding of blood had to be a part of the covering. When Adam and Eve sinned, they lost their close communion with God. But through the blood covenant, God was declaring that their sins were atoned for. The blood one day would bring back the fellowship and joy.

From the time of Adam to the time of Christ, Scripture is filled with accounts of how God entered into blood covenants with His people. **Read** each scriptural account on the following page, and **describe** (✍) what took place to initiate God's blood covenant with man.

Text	Persons(s) Involved	Blood Sacrifice
Genesis 8:20	_____	_____
Genesis 17:10	_____	_____
Exodus 24:8	_____	_____
Genesis 15:1–21	_____	_____
Genesis 31:51–54	_____	_____

The heart attitude of the person making a sacrifice is very important. Over the centuries, Israel became complacent in its sacrifices to God. The hearts of worshipers hardened toward God. Sacrifices that were founded on the blood covenant became customary, ritualistic and routine. Any sacrifice offered to God must be accompanied by a sincere, humble heart before God.

Christ made one final blood sacrifice for us through His death on the cross. Today, our sacrifices involve worship and service. Nevertheless, there are several important principles that we need to understand about sacrificing to God. Some of these principles are listed below. **Read** each Scripture and then, on each line, **write** (✍) the reference from the list below that matches each principle.

> 1 Samuel 15:22–23   Psalm 50:7–15
> Amos 5:21–24   Romans 12:1–3
> Psalm 4:5   Psalm 51:14–17
> John 4:24

The Bible	The sacrifice God desires is . . .
_____	a broken, contrite heart.
_____	given with righteousness.
_____	not given out of rebellion, which is witchcraft.
_____	from true worship in spirit and truth.
_____	living sacrifices—changed lives.
_____	God doesn't need our sacrifices; He desires our thanksgiving and praise.
_____	a sacrifice of righteousness to the Lord.

Ritual without a right heart attitude is empty tradition. God never intended sacrifices to become empty traditions. God takes a blood covenant very seriously. How seriously? He sacrificed His Son as an atonement for our sins. He covers us with the precious blood of Jesus.

What is your heart attitude toward God? Confess any sin, any complacency, any empty tradition in your life. Pray to become a living sacrifice to the Lord. Pray Romans 12:1–2 for your life.

Dear Father, I will, by the mercies of God, present my body as a living sacrifice, holy, acceptable to God, which is my reasonable service. And I will not be conformed to this world, but I will seek to be transformed by the renewing of my mind, that I may prove what is that good and acceptable and perfect will of God. Amen.

THE BLOOD COVENANT

Now Adam knew Eve his wife, and she conceived and bore Cain, and said, 'I have acquired a man from the LORD.' Then she bore again, this time his brother Abel" (Gen. 4:1-2). These two brothers were very different. They chose two different occupations. Abel was a keeper of sheep, but Cain was a tiller of the ground (Gen. 4:2). After what their parents had experienced, it was only natural that the children were taught the principle of presenting gifts to the Lord.

> And in the process of time it came to pass that Cain brought an offering of the fruit of the ground to the LORD. Abel also brought of the firstborn of his flock and of their fat.
>
> —GENESIS 4:3-4

Scripture records that "the Lord respected Abel and his offering, but He did not respect Cain and his offering" (Gen. 4:4-5). What was the difference? Why did God accept one offering and reject the other? The answer is found in Hebrews 11:4. "By faith Abel offered to God a more excellent sacrifice than Cain, through which he obtained witness that he was righteous, God testifying of his gifts; and through it he being dead still speaks."

It was "by faith" that Abel offered a blood sacrifice to the Lord. We know that "faith comes by hearing" (Rom. 10:17), so it's reasonable to assume the two sons knew the power of the blood because their parents shared their experience in the Garden.

How did Abel know to offer a blood sacrifice? I believe Adam and Eve told their sons what God expected. I believe God gave a revelation of the blood covenant to the first man and woman when He sacrificed animals and clothed them with skins that may have been wet with blood (Gen. 3:21). It was a sign of the redemption and deliverance that was to come. No doubt Eve wondered, "Which one of my sons will bruise the serpent's head?" (See Genesis 3:15.)

Both sons knew that God demanded a blood covenant. That is why God asked Cain, "Why are you angry? Why is your face downcast? If you do what is right, will you not be accepted?" (Gen. 4:6-7, NIV). Cain knew what was right, but he didn't do it. Instead he offered a gift of vegetation, and God refused it.

When you give sacrificially to the Lord, what feelings do you have?

_____

_____

_____

_____

_____

Abel was obedient to the Lord. By faith he offered an animal sacrifice—the "firstfruits" of his flock. The substituted blood was given by Abel from a heart of love and trust. Way back in the Garden of Eden, this foreshadowed the need for Christ's death on the cross. Cain offered a gift, but it was not what God required. There is a great difference between presenting what the Lord demands and merely giving a present.

> Has the LORD as great delight in burnt offerings and sacrifices, As in obeying the voice of the LORD? Behold, to obey is better than sacrifice.
>
> —1 SAMUEL 15:22

When you have a softened, humble heart toward God, He accepts the sacrifice of your worship. But a heart hardened by pride and unconfessed sin is unacceptable to God. Is there something keeping your heart from truly worshiping God and sacrificing yourself totally to Him? **Look** over the following list. **Circle** (○) anything that may be keeping you from becoming an obedient, living sacrifice to God. **Describe** (✍) any other hindrances you may have.

Doubt	Unbelief
Unconfessed sin	Other: _____
Pride	Other: _____
Anger	Other: _____

Read 1 John 1:9. Christ offers us total forgiveness from all our sins—if we confess them to Him, He will cleanse us from all unrighteousness. Do not allow a "Cain" attitude to come between you and God. Don't let sin crouch at the door of your life, hindering your sacrifice, your offering and your worship of God.

Write (✍) a prayer confessing anything that may come between you and God. Thank Him for His forgiveness through the blood of Jesus.

_____

_____

_____

THE COVENANT OF PROMISE

One great blood covenant established in the Old Testament is called the Abrahamic covenant.

> The LORD appeared to Abram and said to him, "I am Almighty God; walk before Me and be blameless. And I will make My covenant between Me and you, and will multiply you exceedingly." Then Abram fell on his face, and God talked with him, saying: "As for Me, behold, My covenant is with you, and you shall be a father of many nations. No longer shall your name be called Abram, but your name shall be Abraham; for I have made you a father of many nations."
>
> —GENESIS 17:1-5

Abraham was given a new name by God, and he became a different man. Abraham's relationship to the Lord also changed so much that the Lord would now be called the "God of Abraham." A blood covenant with God transforms lives.

Then God told Abraham, "I will make you exceedingly fruitful; and I will make nations of you, and kings shall come from you. And I will establish My covenant between Me and you and your descendants after you in their generations, for an everlasting covenant, to be God to you and your descendants after you" (vv. 6-7). The Lord also promised to give Abraham and his descendants "the land of Canaan, as an everlasting possession" if they would keep the covenant (vv. 8-9).

Most important, this covenant would be marked by the shedding of blood. "This is My covenant which you shall keep, between Me and you and your descendants after you: Every male child among you shall be circumcised; and you shall be circumcised in the flesh of your foreskins, and it shall be a sign of the covenant between Me and you" (vv. 10-11).

What was the sign of the Abrahamic covenant? Circumcision. Every male child was to have this rite performed when he was eight days old. As a result he would not only enter into the covenant, but he would also take part in God's promises to Abraham.

God honored the covenant so that Abraham, even at his advanced age of nearly one hundred years, was able to father a child. His wife, Sarah, who was ninety, conceived and bore a son. They named him Isaac. After Isaac was born, God chose to test Abraham's faith in the covenant promise to make him the father of a great nation.

How would you feel if God had made such a promise to you and then asked you to sacrifice your child? He asked Abraham to sacrifice Isaac, the child of God's promise. Could you obey such a request?

_____

_____

_____

In Genesis 22, we can read the account where God asks Abraham to take Isaac to Mount Moriah and sacrifice him. Do you think Abraham was being *tested* or *tempted* by God?_____

At times we use these two words—*tempt* and *test*—like synonyms. They are not. (Read James 1:13.) God never tempts us. The purpose of temptation is to cause one to stumble or fall in sin. The purpose of testing is to strengthen and refine as gold one's faith. (See 1 Peter 1:7.)

Could you withstand such a test from God? If God asked you to totally surrender something or someone to Him, could you trust Him enough to do it? Could you trust God totally with an important relationship or other key part of your life? What would be the hardest thing or person for you to surrender to God?

_____

_____

_____

The greatest test of faith is surrender. Some say, "I surrender all," but fail to surrender everything to God." God asks us to say with our whole hearts, "I surrender all."

When they reached the appointed place, Abraham built an altar and placed the wood in order. Isaac must have been filled with faith, too. The Scriptures do not mention any resistance when Abraham "bound Isaac his son and laid him on the altar, upon the wood" (Gen. 22:9). I can only imagine the emotions each of them felt when Abraham "stretched out his hand and took the knife to slay his son.

"But the Angel of the LORD called to him from heaven and said, 'Abraham, Abraham!'

"So he said, 'Here I am.'

"And He said, 'Do not lay your hand on the lad, or do anything to him; for now I know that you fear God, since you have not withheld your son, your only son, from Me'" (vv. 10-12).

Abraham had passed God's test. He chose the Giver over the gift. But the offering of blood still had to be presented. Abraham spotted a ram caught in a thicket that he offered to God.

When we demonstrate our faith in God by our obedience, He not only *promises* to provide for us—He *will* provide! Because of Abraham's faith and obedience, God not only provided the ram caught in a thicket—He fulfilled His promise to make Abraham the father of a great nation.

Are you facing a test of your faith? Is something or someone keeping you from surrendering all to receive the covenant of promise?

Pray the following prayer now:

> *Lord, I surrender _____ to You. I claim*
> *the fullness of Your promises for my life through*
> *Your shed blood. Amen.*

EXODUS AND
THE BLOOD COVENANT

Try to imagine what it must have been like when Moses came down from Mount Sinai to the nearly two million waiting Israelites. Moses told the people what God had declared, and they "answered with one voice and said, 'All the words which the LORD has said we will do'" (Exod. 24:3). It was an important step toward a new blood covenant between God and His people.

Early the next morning Moses built an altar at the foot of the mountain.

> Then he sent young men of the children of Israel, who offered burnt offerings and sacrificed peace offerings of oxen to the LORD. And Moses took half the blood and put it in basins, and half the blood he sprinkled on the altar. Then he took the Book of the Covenant and read in the hearing of the people. And they said, "All that the LORD has said we will do, and be obedient."
>
> —EXODUS 24:5-7

Then, standing before that great multitude, "Moses took the blood, sprinkled it on the people, and said, 'This is the blood of the covenant which the LORD has made with you according to all these words'" (v. 8). Even the written covenant itself was consecrated. The writer of Hebrews says that "he took the blood of calves and goats, with water, scarlet wool, and hyssop, and sprinkled both the book itself and all the people" (Heb. 9:19).

When we honor our covenant with God, God will honor us. Are you honoring your covenant with the living God? One way we honor Him is by obeying His Word.

Here are some truths from the Word about how to know and obey God's Word in your daily life. **Read** each text. **Check (✔)**

each text that you are obeying or applying. **Circle (○)** each text that you need to obey or apply in your life.

❑ "Do not let this Book of the Law depart from your mouth; meditate on it day and night, so that you may be careful to do everything written in it. Then you will be prosperous and successful" (Josh. 1:8, NIV).

❑ "But his delight is in the law of the LORD, and on his law he meditates day and night" (Ps. 1:2, NIV).

❑ "I have hidden your word in my heart that I might not sin against you" (Ps. 119:11, NIV).

❑ "I will always obey your law, for ever and ever" (Ps. 119:44, NIV).

❑ "I will walk about in freedom, for I have sought out your precepts" (Ps. 119:45, NIV).

❑ "Thy word is a lamp unto my feet, and a light unto my path" (Ps. 119:105, KJV).

❑ "If you love me, you will obey what I command" (John 14:15, NIV).

❑ "All Scripture is God-breathed and is useful for teaching, rebuking, correcting, and training in righteousness" (2 Tim. 3:16, NIV).

The remarkable story of Israel's wandering in the desert gives testimony to that fact. "[He] fed you with manna . . . Your garments did not wear out on you, nor did your foot swell these forty years" (Deut. 8:3-4). Why did God protect and provide for the children of Israel? Because they were a covenant people.

Think of all the provisions that God has prospered you with as you keep His covenant. He provides and prospers you under the blood of Jesus Christ. To help you remember how He prospers you, read Psalm 103. Using that psalm as a basis, **list (✍)** the provisions mentioned in the psalm that you are experiencing in your life right now.

_____

_____

_____

_____

_____

What methods are you using to learn God's Word right now in your life? Second Timothy 2:15 advises us to "be diligent to present yourself approved to God, a worker who does not need to be ashamed, rightly dividing the word of truth." Without studying to show ourselves approved of God, we will miss many of God's blessings because of ignorance.

Check (✔) the methods you are using to apply God's Word. Underline the methods you would be willing to begin in order to learn His Word.

❑   A Sunday school class

❑   A worship experience

❑   A Bible study group

❑   Daily individual study

❑   Other: _____

❑   Other: _____

Ask the Holy Spirit to teach you the truths found in God's Word. Go back to the circles you drew earlier around Bible truths that you needed to apply to your life. Spend some time making a prayer covenant with God to apply these truths. Ask Him to provide you with opportunities to become involved in the methods of study that you indicated you would be willing to begin.

WEEK THREE

APPLYING GOD'S BELIEVER PROTECTION PLAN

In 1975, about a year after I began preaching, I had an unusual encounter. After a service held in the home of a pastor friend, I invited those who needed prayer to come forward. One woman brought her teenage daughter. Just as I started to pray, I heard the clear voice of the Lord instruct me to do something I did not understand. He said, "Get the ring off her finger."

I lifted her hand to get a closer look at the silver band around her finger. It had a little snake engraved on it with the head showing and the body coiled around the band. When I glanced back at her, she had a puzzled expression on her face, as if to say, "What difference does it make? Go ahead and pray for me."

I was more bewildered than she was. All I knew was that the Lord had said, "Get the ring off." I can still vividly recall this unusual encounter. I took my thumb and two fingers and tried to slide the ring from her finger. It was a loose-fitting ring, but somehow it would not budge. As I continued to pull, she began to scream. It was a rather loud, terrifying shriek. All the muscles in her body tightened.

Then an ugly, guttural voice spoke through her, chilling me to the marrow. "Leave her alone!" the voice shouted. "She's mine!" The moment I heard those words I knew God had given me the right instructions. Holy anger surged within me because I knew I was in a battle against the power of satan. I continued to pull on the ring. Two of the men in the room could see what was happening, and they held my shoulders as I waged this frightening, but necessary, battle for fifteen to twenty minutes.

Over her screams I finally cried, "I apply the blood of Jesus Christ!" And the moment I said those words the ring came off her finger. Her rigid body relaxed, and her screeching turned into a sigh of relief. She was completely delivered and asked Christ to come into her heart. I believe the power of the blood of Jesus Christ cancels out any covenant made with the power of hell.

You may say, "Benny, do you believe the ring had anything to do with her condition?" Yes. Because that ring symbolized her rebellion against God, I believe it was a symbol of a commitment to the forces of evil.

THIS WEEK'S OVERVIEW

DAY	STUDY TOPIC
ONE	Get Rid of It!
TWO	The Protection of the Blood
THREE	Applying the Blood
FOUR	The Word and the Blood
FIVE	Prayer Power

This week you will discover that the blood of Jesus powerfully protects us from the enemy and defeats the devil's power. You will:

- Learn how the blood protects you.

- Discover help for your household in applying the blood.

- Uncover the hedge of protection available to you as a believer.

- Develop a prayer life of power through the blood.

It's my prayer for you this week that you will discover how to apply the blood for your own life and for your family. Apply the blood daily as you pray. Experience for yourself the mighty power of the blood through prayer.

Memory Verse

Memorize, pray and get into your spirit this word.

The blood shall be to you for a token upon the houses where ye are.

—Exodus 12:13, KJV

GET RID OF IT!

In the famous victory of the Israelites over Jericho, God instructed Joshua to tell his army not to take any of the plunder. He told them to avoid taking Jericho's riches, "lest you become accursed when you take of the accursed things, and make the camp of Israel a curse, and trouble it" (Josh. 6:18).

During their next battle at the city of Ai, Joshua's men were about to be defeated. Joshua tore his clothes and asked the Lord why they were close to defeat. The Lord told him:

> Israel has sinned, and they have also transgressed My covenant which I commanded them. For they have even taken some of the accursed things, and have both stolen and deceived; and they have also put it among their own stuff.
>
> —JOSHUA 7:11

The offending soldier was Achan, of the tribe of Judah. When Joshua confronted him, Achan said, "Indeed I have sinned against the LORD God of Israel, and this is what I have done: When I saw among the spoils a beautiful Babylonian garment, two hundred shekels of silver, and a wedge of gold weighing fifty shekels, I coveted them and took them" (vv. 20–21).

It was only when Achan, his family and the stolen items were destroyed that the curse on Israel was lifted and the covenant restored. Joshua and his men were then able to capture the city of Ai. (See Joshua 7:25; 8:1–28.)

God's message is clear. Be careful of what you allow into your home, for some things bring bondage. For Achan it was a Babylonian garment. For the girl I prayed with, it was a satanic ring. I believe God's protection is lifted when you possess something that goes against His commands. The passage in Joshua 7:10–12 is very clear that you should not have an accursed thing in your home. God said to the children of Israel:

> Neither will I be with you anymore, unless you destroy the accursed from among you.
>
> —JOSHUA 7:12

It's very important that you examine your household to make certain that nothing accursed is under your roof. The following items and activities on this checklist could give the devil a foothold of attack and need to be removed from your house. These things open the door to demonic activity. My strong advice to you is to read your Bible and listen to the voice of the Holy Spirit to avoid these things.

Check (✔) the items and activities on the list below that you have in your home or that you participate in regularly. Add any other things that you believe to be associated with demonic activity.

- ❏ Horoscopes
- ❏ Jewelry with astrological or occult symbols
- ❏ Any books or magazines that contain materials from the occult or New Age movement
- ❏ Pictures that focus on the occult or New Age
- ❏ Phone calls to psychics
- ❏ Watching movies or videos with demonic, occult or New Age themes, or horror films
- ❏ Playing New Age, heavy metal or rock music
- ❏ Playing occult fantasy games
- ❏ Going to séances, palm readings and other such events
- ❏ Becoming involved with cults or false religions
- ❏ Other: _____
- ❏ Other: _____

If you have checked anything on the list above, you need to take the following steps:

1. Get rid of it.

2. Repent and ask the Lord to forgive and cleanse you through His blood.
3. Ask the Holy Spirit to give you the power to resist future temptation
4. Read, study, and memorize God's Word.
5. Rebuke the devil in Jesus' name and apply the blood of Jesus over your home and family.

Circle (◯) any steps you have already taken. <u>Underline</u> the steps you will take immediately.

God's protection is lifted from your life when you open a door to the enemy. These doors are not just the door to demonic activity through the above things. Some of the doors that you may be opening right now could include: (**Check (✔)** any of the following doors that open for the enemy to enter your life.)

❏ Sexual immorality

❏ Physical, sexual or substance abuse

❏ Involvement with the occult

❏ Unconfessed sin

❏ Rebellion against God

Pray right now, confessing your involvement with any item that you have checked. **Read** 1 John 1:5-10 aloud, listening to God's promise to cleanse and forgive us by His blood.

THE PROTECTION
OF THE BLOOD

God sent Moses to warn Pharaoh and the Egyptians that God would send plagues upon them if they did not let His people go. Pharaoh continually refused to let the Hebrews go, until God finally warned He would send a final plague—death to all the firstborn Egyptian males.

Then God told Moses that the time had come for the deliverance of the children of Israel. It was such a momentous event that even their calendar should be changed. The Lord said, "This month shall be your beginning of months; it shall be the first month of the year to you" (Exod. 12:2). God said, "This is your beginning," even though they were leaving a land that had been almost destroyed. The Lord told Moses how the children of Israel would be spared from the death of the firstborn. Each family was to follow these seven instructions:

1. Choose a one-year-old male lamb or goat without blemish (Exod. 12:3-5).
2. Join together with small families that cannot use a whole lamb (Exod. 12:4).
3. Keep the lamb for four days before slaughter (Exod. 12:6).
4. Have the head of the household slay the lamb on the evening of the fourteenth day of the month (Exod. 12:6).
5. Sprinkle the blood of the lamb on the sides and the tops of the door frames of the house (Exod. 12:7).
6. Roast the lamb that evening, and eat it with bitter herbs and unleavened bread (Exod. 12:8).
7. Eat the meal in haste, with your cloaks tucked into your belts, sandals on your feet and staves in your hands (Exod. 12:11).

God told them to prepare because He would pass over the land.

> For I will pass through the land of Egypt on that night, and will strike all the firstborn in the land of Egypt, both man and beast; and against all the gods of Egypt I will execute judgment: I am the LORD.
>
> —EXODUS 12:12

Then the Lord gave this promise:

> Now the blood shall be a sign for you on the houses where you are. And when I see the blood, I will pass over you; and the plague shall not be on you to destroy you when I strike the land of Egypt.
>
> —EXODUS 12:13

At midnight on the night of the Passover, the firstborn in every Egyptian household died. The wailing was heard across the land even before the sun rose (vv. 29-30). But in the houses of the Israelites there was not one dead. That first Passover was a shadow of what was to happen one day on a hill called Calvary. For at Calvary "Christ, our Passover, has been sacrificed" (1 Cor. 5:7, NIV). There we were "redeemed with the precious blood of Christ, as of a lamb without blemish and without spot" (1 Pet. 1:19).

Why did the Lord tell the Israelites to find a lamb for each household (Exod. 12:3)? I believe it is because the blessings of God's covenant can lead to salvation for an entire family (1 Cor. 7:14).

God has intervened to bring salvation to an entire family many times. The Bible gives us several examples. **Read** the following passages and **describe** (✍) what God said to righteous people about saving their households. Write down the name of the individual to whom God spoke.

Text	Individual	God's Words
Genesis 7:1	_____	_____
Genesis 19:29	_____	_____
Acts 16:30-31	_____	_____
1 Corinthians 7:14	_____	_____

I believe the Lord places special grace and protection on an entire home because of one person who comes into His kingdom. Just as the ancient Israelites put the blood of the Passover lamb on their doorposts to protect their families, so you can apply the blood of Jesus to your family, covering them with God's grace and help.

Below is an illustration of a doorpost with the blood of Christ applied to it. Inside the door opening, write the names of family members whom you are now praying for and covering with the blood of Jesus.

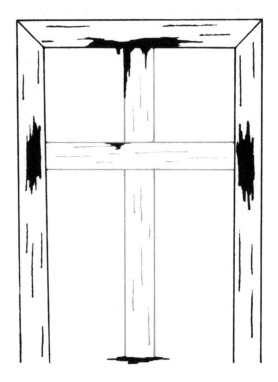

Look at each name you have written in the doorway. Now pray this prayer for each person:

Lord, I cover _____ with the blood of Jesus. Protect that person, Lord, for Your name's sake. Amen.

DAY 3

APPLYING THE BLOOD

When you ask God to cover your family with the blood of His Son, I believe the Lord then builds a hedge of protection around your home. That is what He did for Job.

The Bible states that Job was a righteous man, "blameless and upright, and one who feared God and shunned evil" (Job 1:1). God made him a prosperous man, with thousands of sheep, camels, oxen and other possessions. He was called "the greatest of all the people of the East" (v. 3).

But Job was concerned about the lifestyles of his children. His seven sons would take turns holding feasts in their homes, and they would invite their three sisters to eat and drink with them.

Job was so troubled about their spiritual condition that when the days of feasting were over, "Job would send and sanctify them, and he would rise early in the morning and offer burnt offerings according to the number of them all. For Job said, 'It may be that my sons have sinned and cursed God in their hearts.' Thus Job did regularly" (v. 5).

One day some angels presented themselves to the Lord, and satan was among them.

> And the LORD said to Satan, "From where do you come?"
> So Satan answered the LORD and said, "From going to and fro on the earth, and from walking back and forth on it."
>
> Then the LORD said to Satan, "Have you considered My servant Job, that there is none like him on the earth, a blameless and upright man, one who fears God and shuns evil?"
>
> So Satan answered the LORD and said, "Does Job fear God for nothing? Have You not made a hedge around him, around his household, and around all that he has on every side?"
>
> —JOB 1:7–10

Job did exactly what God had instructed. He applied the blood, and he did it "regularly" (v. 5). Job covered his family with the blood by sacrificing.

In the New Testament the sacrifice has been made once and for all through Jesus Christ. We can take advantage of what He has done for us. God will honor our faith as we learn to cover our families with the blood of Christ.

Are you, like Job, applying the blood and building a hedge about your family? In 2 Corinthians 4:13 we are advised, "Since we have the same spirit of faith . . . we also believe and therefore speak." Applying the blood is not a magic formula or phrase. The power of the blood is activated by faith in Jesus. By faith we believe in the sacrifice Christ made, in the blood He already shed. Our belief motivates us to speak it to God in prayer.

Now, I don't pray and apply the blood every day out of a sense of duty or compulsion. I pray out of love for the Lord and the desire to fellowship continually with the Holy Spirit. In prayer, I apply the blood of Jesus Christ to my family and life situations. What does that mean? Simply this: We appropriate all of the benefits of the cross of Jesus Christ.

Listed below are some of the benefits available to believers through the shed blood of Jesus on the cross of Calvary. **Look up** each Scripture reference and **draw a line** from that reference to the benefit listed in that verse. Check your answers with the answer key below when you have finished.

John 6:54	Peace
1 Corinthians 1:18	Access
Galatians 3:13–14	Eternal life
Ephesians 2:16	The power of God
Ephesians 2:18	Ability to overcome the enemy
Colossians 1:20	The promise of the Spirit
Hebrews 10:19	Reconciliation
Revelation 12:11	Boldness to enter the holiest

ANSWER KEY: John 6:54, eternal life; 1 Cor. 1:18, the power of God; Gal. 3:13–14, the promise of the Spirit; Eph. 2:16, reconciliation; Eph. 2:18, access; Col. 1:20, peace; Heb. 10:19, boldness to enter the holiest; Rev. 12:11, ability to overcome the enemy

The blood does not cover you automatically. God does not reach down from the sky and place the blood mark on your dwelling place. We have to ask for His protection. Remember, God supplies, but we apply through our believing prayer. The children of Israel took the blood "and put it on the two doorposts and on the lintel of the houses" (Exod. 12:7).

Where do you need to apply the blood over your relationships and your possessions? Using the list below of benefits available through the blood of Jesus, think of a person you know who needs each benefit. List that person's name by the benefit and then **pray** to apply the blood to that person's life.

Name	I apply the blood that they may know God's:
_____	Protection
_____	Forgiveness
_____	Security in God's grace
_____	Reconciliation
_____	Cleansing
_____	Sanctification
_____	Presence
_____	Victory

Take the time now to **pray** for each person that you named. Expect each person to experience Christ's grace and victory in their lives because of the covering of His blood.

THE WORD
AND THE BLOOD

The Word of God is indispensable to our knowledge and to our faith in God. We need to gain the greatest knowledge of the Word that is possible. The Word and the blood work together. The Word *says,* and the blood *does.*

The evil one may fight you at every turn, but when you apply the blood, God's power comes alive. As a minister, I have preached on countless topics, but each time I preach on the blood, three things happen.

- Satan makes every attempt to distract me from my preparation on the topic.

- The devil tries his best to disturb the people gathered in the meeting place to hear my message.

- An unusually powerful presence of the Lord accompanies the message, and a large number of people find Christ as Savior.

Describe (✍) below how the enemy attacks you when you speak about the blood of Jesus or seek to apply the blood to your life or to someone else's life.

_____

_____

_____

Just as some ministers have never preached a sermon on the blood, some Christians have rarely uttered the word *blood* since their conversions. The subject seems to be totally erased from their minds. But God specifically instructed the Israelites to observe the Passover "as an ordinance for you and your sons forever" (Exod. 12:24). Forever means *forever.*

Put a check (✔) in the appropriate box below each statement.

When was the last time you:

1. Told someone about the shed blood of Jesus?

   ❏ Recently   ❏ Not long ago

   ❏ Several months ago   ❏ Never

2. Spoke the Word to defeat the enemy?

   ❏ Recently   ❏ Not long ago

   ❏ Several months ago   ❏ Never

3. Prayed and applied the blood of Christ to a person, place or situation?

   ❏ Recently   ❏ Not long ago

   ❏ Several months ago   ❏ Never

If you checked the "several months ago" or "never" boxes, will you make the decision now to start responding more often in these ways?

Here are some important verses from the Word that you can use to speak to the enemy to claim victory over his attacks. **Summarize** what each verse says to the enemy.

The Word	To the enemy I declare:
Psalm 52:5	_____
Romans 16:20	_____
Ephesians 6:10–13	_____
James 4:7–10	_____
1 John 3:8; 4:4	_____

The enemy's weapons cannot succeed. The devil is under your feet. You have the full armor of God available to defend against his attacks. With humility, you can resist his every move. Satan has already been defeated and his works destroyed at the cross by the shed blood of Jesus Christ. God's Spirit within you is greater than the prince of this world.

Read again the summaries you wrote of these verses. Now **write** (✍) a prayer using these verses to defeat the enemy and claim victory by the blood of Jesus Christ over any attack from the enemy you now face.

_____

_____

_____

_____

_____

_____

_____

_____

PRAYER POWER

The Lord has never changed His mind about His blood covenant with His people. It was not limited to the forty years that the children of Israel journeyed to the Promised Land. The command was in effect even after they reached their destination. "It will come to pass when you come to the land which the LORD will give you, just as He promised, that you shall keep this service" (Exod. 12:25).

We have even more to celebrate. God replaced the blood of sheeps and goats with the perfect sacrifice, the blood of His Son. By the same token we are to celebrate His covenant forever.

You may ask, "Benny, how often should we ask God to cover us with the blood?"

I personally do it every time I pray. There is not a day that I do not in prayer say, "Lord, cover Suzanne, Jessica, Natasha, Joshua and Eleasha with Your blood." I do the same thing with each one of them separately. If I'm traveling, I call them on the phone and pray with them and continually pray that nothing will come into their hearts and minds but what is of the Lord.

Several years ago I overheard my Tasha praying. She didn't know I was listening. I put my head to the door that was opened slightly. I was moved as I heard her saying, "Now, Lord, You shed Your blood for us, and I ask You to cover all of us." And she prayed for us one by one. There was another time when she said, "Now, satan, you hear me real good: You can't touch me. The blood is covering me."

That's why it's so wonderful when parents ask the Lord to protect their children with the blood. Their children not only copy them but will ask questions about it. Then the parents have the opportunity to tell their children what the Lord has done.

My daughter Tasha is now attending a university. Yet, I can still remember when she reached the age to ask, "Daddy, why do you do that?" I was able to tell them about the Passover story and how the blood of Jesus has been shed for us.

Now is the time for you to put your faith into action. **Pray.** Ask the Lord to cover, protect and give you victory through the blood. **Complete (✎)** the following sentences, inserting the names and needs of your family.

*   I ask the Lord through His blood to cleanse _____

    _____.

*   I ask the Lord through His blood to forgive _____

    _____.

*   I ask the Lord by His blood to cover _____

    _____.

*   I ask the Lord by His blood to protect_____

    _____.

*   I ask victory through Jesus' blood for _____

    _____.

How is your prayer power? Do you pray in power through the blood of Christ, or do you simply utter vain repetitions to God?

E. M. Bounds, a turn-of-the-century preacher who is well known for his books on prayer, said, "Only God can move mountains, but faith and prayer move God."* I believe that prayer is faith passing into action. Only as we pray and trust, by faith, in the blood of Jesus, will the mountains that we face in our lives move.

No matter what obstacles you may be facing today, as you pray in faith that mountain will be removed. Take a moment to write down the problems you are facing today. Then, in prayer command them to be removed in Jesus' name as you apply the blood to each situation.

_____

_____

_____

* *The Best of E. M. Bounds on Prayer* (Grand Rapids, MI: Baker Book House, 1981), 27.

_____

_____

_____

_____

_____

_____

Now **write** (✍) a prayer thanking Jesus for His shed blood.

_____

_____

_____

_____

_____

_____

There's Cleansing in the Blood

When God gave the ordinances in the Old Testament, He spoke to Moses regarding "the law of the leper for the day of his cleansing" (Lev. 14:2).

In Scripture, leprosy refers to a variety of skin diseases. It is also a symbol of sin. So the cleansing of the leper foreshadowed God's future plan to cleanse all of mankind from sin.

During your study on the blood this week, you will:

- Discover the cleansing power of the blood.

- Understand how the cleansing of the leper in the Old Testament represents your cleansing at the cross.

- Learn about the relationship between the blood and the Holy Spirit.

- Explore the power of the anointing of the Holy Spirit released by the shed blood of Jesus.

It is my prayer this week that the Holy Spirit will fill and empower you through the precious blood of our Savior. Be ready to welcome the Holy Spirit into your daily walk with Jesus. Be prepared to be set free from the chains of bondage in your life.

THIS WEEK'S OVERVIEW

DAY	STUDY TOPIC
ONE	Christ's Blood Shed for Cleansing
TWO	The Blood and the Spirit
THREE	A Mighty Wind
FOUR	The Blood and the Anointing
FIVE	Sprinkled and Poured

Memory Verse

As you study this week, memorize and say aloud often this scripture:

> Elect according to the foreknowledge of God the Father,
> in sanctification of the Spirit, for obedience and sprink-
> ling of the blood of Jesus Christ.
>
> —1 PETER 1:2

Also as you study this week, remember that you are one of the elect, a saint of the Most High God being sanctified by the Spirit and sprinkled by the blood.

CHRIST'S BLOOD
SHED FOR CLEANSING

The cleansing of the leper in the Old Testament (Lev. 14:2) foreshadowed God's future plan to cleanse all of mankind from sin by the blood of Christ. Today we will take a look at the similarities between the cleansed leper and the cleansed sinner.

Read each Scripture portion listed below. **Discuss** the similarities and symbolism of each step in the process of cleansing.

Scripture	Symbolic Action in the OT	Christ's Sacrifice in the NT
Leviticus 14:2	The leper to be cleansed is brought to the priest.	The unbeliever is brought to an awareness of his need for God.
Leviticus 14:4	The priest was instructed to go outside the city, taking: two living and clean birds,	Jesus was crucified outside the walls of Jerusalem. Symbolizes the Lord's death and resurrection.
	cedar wood	Points to the cross on which Jesus died.
	scarlet,	Symbolizes His suffering and shed blood.
	hyssop	Symbolizes faith (Ps. 51:7).

The hyssop that was used in purification ceremonies is generally considered to be a fragrant plant from the marjoram family. It symbolizes faith to me because it was used in the application of the blood (Exod. 12:22).

What happened next was amazing in light of what Christ would do at Calvary.

> Then the priest shall order that one of the birds be killed over fresh water in a clay pot. He is then to take the live bird and dip it, together with the cedar wood, the scarlet yarn and the hyssop, into the blood of the bird that was killed over the fresh water.
>
> —LEVITICUS 14:5-6, NIV

Scripture	Symbolic Action in the OT	Christ's Sacrifice in the NT
Leviticus 13:5-6	The blood of the first bird is caught in an earthen vessel.	Christ shed His blood in an earthen vessel— His human body.
	The living bird was dipped in the blood of the bird that was killed over the fresh water.	Symbolizes the sinner's cleansing by the Word (Eph. 5:26).
	This bird was dipped with the cedar wood, scarlet yarn, and the hyssop.	Symbolizes the work of the cross of Christ, His suffering and our faith.

Scripture	Symbolic Action in the OT	Christ's Sacrifice in the NT
Leviticus 14:7	The leper was sprinkled with the blood and water seven times from the living bird.	Symbolizes the act of our sins being cleansed by the blood of Christ.
	The living bird was released in the open fields.	The sinner is resurrected unto new life.
Leviticus 14:8	The cleansed leper was allowed to enter the camp.	The sinner who has been purified by the blood of Christ is ready to enter God's kingdom.

Because of the blood of Jesus, the floodgates of God's anointing can be released through His Holy Spirit in our lives. As you think about the scene of the crucifixion, what feelings and thoughts do you have?

Using the following descriptive feelings (and any others of your own), **write** a prayer **describing** (✍) your own reaction as you reflect on the act of Jesus shedding His blood for you.

Awe	Forgiveness	Mercy
Thanksgiving	Healing	Liberation
Shame	Power	Freedom
Love	Cleansing	Justice

Dear Jesus,
When I think about YOU shedding Your blood for ME . . .

_____

_____

_____

THE BLOOD
AND THE SPIRIT

When the Holy Spirit became my closest friend, comforter and guide, God began to reveal to me through His Word that it was the shed blood of Christ that made it possible for the Holy Spirit to descend.

On the Day of Pentecost Peter spoke of the Lord's death and resurrection. He continued: "Therefore being exalted to the right hand of God, and having received from the Father the promise of the Holy Spirit, He poured out this which you now see and hear" (Acts 2:33).

Remember that the Lord purchased man's redemption by His atoning death and resurrection, then ascended to His Father and there presented the blood, which was the evidence of redemption.

> But Christ came as High Priest of the good things to come, with the greater and more perfect tabernacle not made with hands, that is, not of this creation. Not with the blood of goats and calves, but with His own blood He entered the Most Holy Place once for all, having obtained eternal redemption.
>
> —HEBREWS 9:11–12

When the Father accepted the blood, I believe Christ Jesus received from the Father the gift of the Holy Spirit to pour out upon those who believed in Him.* And now the Holy Spirit is within us to enable us to live the Christian life. In the following scripture, <u>underline</u> the words that describe what you need the most in your life. Speaking through Ezekiel, God said:

> I will give you a new heart and put a new spirit within you; I will take the heart of stone out of your flesh and give you a heart of flesh. I will put My Spirit within you

---

* Derek Prince, *The Spirit-Filled Believer's Handbook* (Lake Mary, FL: Charisma House, 1993), 251.

and cause you to walk in My statutes, and you will keep My judgments and do them.

—EZEKIEL 36:26-27

The Holy Spirit not only enables us to live the Christian life but will also make God's presence very real to us. "And I will not hide My face from them anymore; for I shall have poured out My Spirit on the house of Israel, says the Lord GOD" (Ezek. 39:29).

My first encounter with the Holy Spirit was glorious. Even though I had never experienced anything like that before, I should not have been surprised when my life was completely transformed by the power of the Holy Spirit. That is exactly what happens when you meet the Spirit of God. The prophet Samuel described it to Saul this way: "Then the Spirit of the LORD will come upon you, and you will prophesy with them and be turned into another man" (1 Sam. 10:6).

Only after the blood of Jesus cleanses and sanctifies us can the Holy Spirit enter our lives. Remember, God is holy. As the temple of the Holy Spirit, our bodies must be cleansed and purified by the blood. Peter instructed the crowd on the day of Pentecost to "repent, and let every one of you be baptized in the name of Jesus Christ for the remission of sins; and you shall receive the gift of the Holy Spirit" (Acts 2:38). When we repent of our sin and confess Jesus as our Lord and Savior, His blood cleanses us as a vessel for His Holy Spirit.

Once the Holy Spirit begins working in your life, how does He minister to you? **Read** the following scriptures. **Describe (✍)** what each text says about the ministry of the Holy Spirit in your life.

The Word	The Work of the Holy Spirit
1 Samuel 10:6	_____
Ezekiel 39:26-29	_____
Matthew 3:11	_____
John 14:15-31	_____
John 16:5-15	_____
Acts 1:7-8; 2:1-21	_____
1 Corinthians 12:1-11	_____

Galatians 5:16-23 _____

Ephesians 5:18-19 _____

1 John 3:24-4:10; 5:6-13 _____

Look over the passages you have just read. **Circle** (◯) the passage that means the most to you. <u>Underline</u> the work of the Spirit that you need most in your life.

Now **write** (✐) a prayer asking the Father in Jesus' name to send His Holy Spirit to fill and empower you to be changed by His Presence.

_____

_____

_____

A MIGHTY WIND

Is it really possible that the Holy Spirit can change us totally? Absolutely. If the Lord could turn mud into man as He breathed the breath of life into him, think what He can do by breathing on us again! That is what happened at Pentecost. "And suddenly there came a sound from heaven, as of a rushing mighty wind, and it filled the whole house where they were sitting" (Acts 2:2).

Those who gathered in the upper room felt the breath of almighty God. And they were transformed. When the Holy Spirit empowers your life, you can expect three things to happen:

1. The Lord will become very close to you.

I hear so many people express a desire to get closer to God, to have a closer, more intimate relationship with Him. What ways can we use to try to get closer to God? **Check (✔)** the ways you have used to try to get closer to God. Add additional ways you have tried.

❏ Read my Bible

❏ Go to church more often

❏ Try to be more obedient to His Word

❏ Pray more

❏ Serve Him more

❏ Other: _____

❏ Other: _____

God has already revealed to us the way to enter a closer relationship with Him. **Read** James 4:7–8 and **describe (✍)** how to get closer to God.

_____

_____

_____

- When we enter a closer relationship with God, our ulti-mate desire will be to walk in the ways of God. The ultimate desire of my life right now is

_____

- You will be miraculously transformed into a new person. One way the Holy Spirit has transformed my life is

_____

2. The Holy Spirit will come to dwell within you.

I am convinced that the Holy Spirit, alive and present on the earth today, is the sign of the covenant God has made with us through the blood of His Son Jesus.

> In Him you also trusted, after you heard the word of truth, the gospel of your salvation; in whom also, having believed, you were sealed with the Holy Spirit of promise, who is the guarantee of our inheritance until the redemption of the purchased possession, to the praise of His glory.
>
> —EPHESIANS 1:13-14

In the blood of Christ, all the promises of God are fulfilled and completed. His Spirit seals those promises in our lives. Read 2 Corinthians 1:20-22. Describe (✍) how God fulfills His promises to us.

_____

_____

_____

I have met many people who pray, "Lord, send the Holy Spirit into my life! Fill me with Your power!" The Holy Spirit will come when we honor the death of Jesus Christ and His blood.

In fact, when we repent and are cleansed by His blood, the Holy

Spirit comes to dwell within us. **Read** each of the following verses and **describe** (✍) what the verse says about the dwelling place of God.

Text	God's Dwelling Place . . .
1 Corinthians 3:16–17	_____
1 Corinthians 6:19–20	_____
2 Corinthians 6:16	_____
Ephesians 2:21-22	_____

3. God's Spirit will breathe life into you.

Not only does the Holy Spirit come to dwell within us, transforming us into the dwelling of God, but God's Spirit breathes life into that dwelling place. In Hebrew, the word for God's Spirit literally means "breath, wind." We merely exist until God's Spirit indwells us. There is no true life within us until the blood of Jesus Christ cleanses us from all sin and the Holy Spirit breathes His life into us (John 10:10; 14:1–6).

Write (✍) a prayer thanking Jesus for shedding His blood, cleansing you and transforming you into the dwelling place of the Holy Spirit.

_____

_____

_____

DAY 4

THE BLOOD AND
THE ANOINTING

Every day I thank God for the blood of Christ. Because the blood was shed for our sins, the Holy Spirit came, and today we can know God's anointing on our lives and work. When we are empowered by the oil of the Holy Spirit, we are freed from the chains of bondage. Every time I am touched by the power of God I feel like the psalmist who declared, "Let God arise, let His enemies be scattered" (Ps. 68:1).

Earlier in our study we discovered how the blood brought cleansing to the leper, who symbolized sinful man. But that was only the beginning. Look what happened to the leper next. The blood made it possible for him to be anointed.

When a man was allowed back in the camp (Lev. 14:8), he was directed to "take two male lambs without blemish, one ewe lamb of the first year without blemish, three-tenths of an ephah of fine flour mixed with oil as a grain offering, and one log [about two-thirds of a pint] of oil" (Lev. 14:10).

The priest was to "take one male lamb and offer it as a trespass offering" (Lev. 14:12)—as a restitution for a specific sin. "Then he shall kill the lamb in the place where he kills the sin offering and the burnt offering, in a holy place" (Lev. 14:13).

Did you notice that the man offered more sacrifices even after he was considered cleansed and allowed back into the camp? In the same way, the Lord Jesus shed His blood once for the remission of our sins, but we continue to ask for the cleansing and protection that His blood provides. The Lord Jesus even taught His disciples to say in prayer: "And forgive us our debts, as we forgive our debtors. And do not lead us into temptation, but deliver us from the evil one" (Matt. 6:12–13).

Just as the blood of Jesus cleanses us and protects us, it also provides us access to the anointing of God upon our lives to enable us to serve God. God told Moses: "You shall anoint them . . . that they may minister to Me as priests" (Exod. 40:15).

In my own ministry I am always aware of the fact that what God is doing He is doing because of His anointing. Without it I would be spiritually bankrupt. My daily prayer is, "Lord, please don't ever lift Your anointing from me. I'd rather die than lose Your wonderful presence upon my life."

The Book of Psalms often speaks of "the Lord's anointed." While these verses point to the coming of our Messiah, Jesus Christ, they also speak of the blessings associated with the anointing of God. **Read** each verse, and **describe** (✍) the blessings each verse gives for the believer who has access through Christ's blood and the indwelling Holy Spirit to the anointing of God.

Verse	Blessing of the Anointing
Psalm 15:50	
Psalm 20:6	
Psalm 45:7	
Psalm 84:9	
Psalm 92:10	
Psalm 105:15	
Psalm 132:17	

Now think about the circumstances of your own life as you read the list one more time. **<u>Underline</u>** the blessings of the anointing of God that you see evident in your own life. **Circle (◯)** the blessings that are most needed in your life.

Remember that as you walk in obedience to God, you don't have to fear losing the anointing. You can look forward to God's blessings instead.

Pray this prayer:

Lord Jesus, cover me with Your precious blood, which cleanses me from sin. Holy Spirit, fill my life and prepare me to be a dwelling place for You, dear Lord. Father, cover me with the blood of Your own Son and grant me access to the blessings of heaven. Anoint me from the top of my head to the tip of my toes that I may be dedicated fully to You, wonderful Lord. Amen.

SPRINKLED AND POURED

After the priest applied blood to the leper, God said, "Now it is time for the anointing." The leper had been cleansed by the blood. Now it was time for him to receive an anointing with oil. The priest was instructed to take "some of the log of oil, and pour it into the palm of his own left hand. Then the priest shall dip his right finger in the oil that is in his left hand, and shall sprinkle some of the oil with his finger seven times before the Lord" (Lev. 14:15-16).

The anointing oil throughout Scripture represents the work of the Holy Spirit in consecrating and empowering a person for service. It is essential to understand that God anoints what the blood has covered. The anointing of the Holy Spirit *follows* the blood. The anointing oil was sprinkled seven times—God's number of completion—to represent the reception of a total anointing.

I believe the anointing multiplies the benefits of the blood of Christ, enabling the believer to live an overcoming, victorious life. The leper had been sprinkled with blood on his right ear, right thumb, and big toe. Now the priest places the anointing oil on top of the blood (Lev. 14:17). It is the same in the believer's life— where you find the blood of the cross, you will find the anointing of the Holy Spirit.

- When the blood is applied to our hearing, we will not hear the enemy's voice. Then God anoints our ears so we can hear His voice. (See Jeremiah 6:10; Revelation 2:7.)

- When the blood is applied to our hands, the devil cannot touch our work for God. But when God anoints our hands, the anointing multiplies our efforts. (See Psalm 90:17.)

- When the blood is applied to our walk, then God anoints our steps so that we can walk with Him. (See Romans 6:4; 8:1.)

We have been redeemed and washed by the blood, but our walk needs to be cleansed by His Word every day because our lives constantly touch the dirt of the world (Eph. 5:26).

Examine your life. On the lines below, **describe** (✍) how the cleansing of the blood and the anointing of the Holy Spirit can help you in each of these three areas.

My hearing (thought life, mind and emotions)

_____

_____

My hands (work, career and job)

_____

_____

My walk (spiritual disciplines, relationship with others and with the Lord)

_____

_____

As Christians we are touching the world every day. That's why we need to come back to the Lord daily and say, "Cleanse me anew, and wash me again." **Pray** these words aloud right now. Let the enemy hear your declaration.

In the story of the priest cleansing the leper (Lev. 14) there was one final step. The priest was instructed:

> The rest of the oil that is in the priest's hand he shall put on the head of him who is to be cleansed. So the priest shall make atonement for him before the Lord.
>
> —LEVITICUS 14:18

God wants to cover us totally from head to toe with the oil of His Spirit—our thoughts, our sight, our words and our entire lives. Not only do we have the atonement of the blood, but we have the anointing of the Holy Spirit. Paul reminded the Corinthians:

Now He who establishes us with you in Christ and has anointed us is God, who also has sealed us and given us the Spirit in our hearts as a guarantee.

—1 CORINTHIANS 1:21–22

We have the anointing of the Holy Spirit as God's guarantee. The word *guarantee* comes from the Hebrew word *arrhaabon,* which means "a pledge, money or property given in advance as security for the rest."

What a promise! Because of Christ's atoning blood and the Spirit's anointing we have "security for the rest." As Paul also reminded the Corinthians, "Eye hath not seen, nor ear heard, neither have entered into the heart of man, the things which God hath prepared for them that love Him" (1 Cor. 2:9, KJV).

Write (✍) a prayer thanking God for the atonement of the blood and the anointing of the Spirit upon your life. Let Him anoint and cleanse you with His blood and Spirit from head to toe. Write that prayer here:

_____

_____

_____

There's New Life in the Blood

Once a year on the Day of Atonement, the High Priest would enter the holy of holies and sprinkle the blood of the atonement on the mercy seat of the ark. This sprinkling of blood would be for the sins of God's people to be forgiven. Hebrews 9:7 declares:

> But only the high priest entered the inner room, and that only once a year, and never without blood, which he offered for himself for the sins the people had committed in ignorance.
>
> —NIV

You and I have a unique privilege as a "royal priesthood" (1 Peter 2:9). Through the blood of Jesus poured out for us on the cross, we can enter the holy of holies any time, any place, for any reason. Boldly we come before God with the petitions for our families, our friends, our fellow saints and any person for whom the Holy Spirit leads us to intercede, bringing that person's needs to Him.

As you study this week, you will:

- Understand how the blood of Jesus cleanses from past guilt.

- Develop the foundations for a clear conscience.

- Learn what you have been redeemed from and to.

- See how the blood of Jesus reconciles us to God, the Father.

I pray that as you study this week, any bondage of past guilt and sin will be broken in Jesus' name.

THIS WEEK'S OVERVIEW

DAY	STUDY TOPIC
ONE	A Forgiven Past in the Blood
TWO	A Clear Conscience
THREE	Bought With a Price
FOUR	Redeemed to . . .
FIVE	Reconciled by the Blood

Memory Verse

Memorize and get this Word in you!

For you were bought at a price; therefore glorify God in your body and your spirit, which are God's.

—1 CORINTHIANS 6:20

DAY 1

A FORGIVEN PAST
IN THE BLOOD

Millions of people live in a never-ending cycle of hope-lessness and despair because they cannot forget about yesterday. They are tormented by memories that can lead to depression, mental anguish and even suicide.

Satan is aware of our weaknesses. That is why he uses our past mistakes to torture and trap us. The devil's greatest weapon against us is our past. But when you understand the work of the cross and the power of the blood, those dead works will be removed from your conscience.

> For if the blood of bulls and of goats, and the ashes of an heifer sprinkling the unclean, sanctifieth to the purifying of the flesh: how much more shall the blood of Christ, who through the eternal Spirit offered Himself without spot to God, purge your conscience from dead works to serve the living God?
>
> —HEBREWS 9:13–14, KJV

Do you realize how liberating it is to be freed from your past? Can you comprehend fully what it means to live without guilt or condemnation? You may think your past is especially blemished compared to those around you. But R. A. Torrey says, "If we could see our past as God sees it before it is washed, the record of the best of us would be black, black, black. But if we are walking in the light, submitting to the truth of God, believing in the light, in Christ, our record today is [as] white as Christ's garments were when the disciples saw Him on the Mount of Transfiguration. (See Matthew 17:2; Mark 9:3; Luke 9:29.)"*

Let these words sink into your heart: *The moment the shed blood of Christ has been applied to your heart, your past is buried. It is*

* R. A. Torrey, *How to Obtain Fullness of Power* (Tarrytown, NY: Fleming H. Revell Company, 1897; Murfreesboro, TN: Sword of the Lord Publishers, n.d.), 19.

gone forever and no longer remembered in glory. To dwell on it is an insult to God.

The following passages reveal God's methods of dealing with our sin. They also reveal the actions we must take before God can deal with our sin. **Read** these passages, and **describe** (✍) what we must do about our sin and what each verse says God will do to deal with our sin problem.

Verse	My Part	God's Part
Psalm 103:8-12		
Isaiah 1:18-20		
Isaiah 43:25-26		
Matthew 6:14-15		
Romans 5:8-9		
Romans 8:1-2		
1 John 1:7-9		

The Word of God declares that when we confess our sins, God will forgive us of our sins and cleanse us from all unrighteousness. Many, however, insult the work of the cross and our wonderful Lord Jesus when they continually revisit the guilt of their past. Jesus Christ took our sins upon Himself, died on the cross and shed His blood to cleanse you and me. Yet many Christians find it hard to forget about their past sin and failure. Remember Jesus convicts of sin; the accuser wants us to feel guilty about sin so that he can render our lives and testimonies powerless to those who know us. Think about your own life. On the lines below, list any unconfessed sin from the past about which you still feel guilt and pain.

Confessed Sin I Still Feel Guilty About...

_____

_____

_____

Now let the pencil or pen that you are using represent the love and mercy of God. God in His love and mercy forgives and forgets your sin when you confess it. The blood completely cleanses you and sets you free from past guilt and shame. Take your pencil or pen and, in big letters, **write** (✍) "FORGIVEN" across each line. As you do, release that guilt to the cleansing blood of Jesus Christ, and live in the forgiveness available to you through the mercy and love of God. This is how God sees your sin once the blood has been applied to your life. Pray and thank Jesus for His shed blood as you do this.

If you continue to feel guilty about past sin it's because you choose to do so as a result of listening to the lies of your accuser, the devil. The devil will try to steal your joy with his constant accusations. Don't let him. Rebuke him. Silence him through the name and blood of Jesus Christ.

Whenever you feel condemned by others, by the world or by satan over sins that you have put under the blood, pray this prayer:

Lord Jesus, I thank You for Your shed blood. Thank You for forgiving me of all my sin. In Your name I silence the devil's accusations. I declare that I am cleansed by Your blood. Praise You, wonderful Jesus. Amen.

A CLEAR CONSCIENCE

Imagine yourself in a courtroom. God is the judge, and you are standing before Him. In the presence of His holiness, you are overwhelmed by a relentless consciousness of your sin. God's voice thunders out, "I know you are guilty."

You tremble before the holy and righteous Judge, knowing you deserve the sentence of death. Then God continues, "You are guilty, but I declare you righteous. Your punishment is waived."

That is called *justification*. God gives you a new legal standing. Your slate is wiped clean. God declares you righteous because of what Jesus has done.

The sins of your past cannot be erased simply because you want them to be. You cannot be freed from a sinful life by merely saying, "I'm going to forget about it."

God said He would "purge" us. The blood will purge your conscience completely—not only your transgressions, but every thought connected with them. Nothing but the blood of Christ can cleanse your mind from thoughts of past and present sins. Since we have "a High Priest over the house of God, let us draw near with a true heart in full assurance of faith, having our hearts sprinkled from an evil conscience" (Heb. 10:21-22).

An evil conscience remembers yesterday and whispers, "You're a sinner."

But in heaven the Lord says, "Welcome! I have delivered you from your iniquities. You are forgiven. Only saints can enter here, and the blood has made you righteous."

To many it sounds impossible that we can stand before God with the righteousness of Christ, but it is true. Because the blood of Jesus is pure, we become pure in God's sight. The Lord cleanses our minds from the past and the present. That is why I love to sing, "There is power, power, wonder-working power in the precious blood of the Lamb."

By His promise you can now say, "The blood has washed my past, and I am free!"

Now say that aloud. Shout it. Write it down and put it on your mirror or refrigerator to remind you constantly that you are forgiven.

Psalm 51 is an important psalm of confession and forgiveness. As you **read** the psalm, **write** (✍) your name on each blank line. Announce to the enemy that you are forgiven. As you **pray** the words of this psalm, allow the cleansing blood of Jesus to wash you white as snow.

Praying Psalm 51

Have mercy upon (me) _____, O God, according to Your lovingkindness; according unto the multitude of Your tender mercies, blot out my transgressions. Wash me thoroughly from my iniquity, and cleanse me from my sin. For I acknowledge my transgressions, and my sin is always before me. Against You, You only, has _____ sinned, and done this evil in Your sight—that You may be found just when You speak, and blameless when You judge.

Behold, (I) _____ was brought forth in iniquity; and in sin my mother conceived me. Behold, You desire truth in the inward parts, and in the hidden part You will make me to know wisdom. Purge me with hyssop, and I shall be clean; wash me, and _____ shall be whiter than snow. Make (me) _____ [to] hear joy and gladness, that the bones You have broken may rejoice. Hide Your face from my sins, and blot out all my iniquities.

Create in (me) _____ a clean heart, O God, and renew a steadfast spirit within me. Do not cast (me) _____ away from Your presence, and do not take Your Holy Spirit from (me) _____. Restore to (me) the joy of Your salvation, and uphold (me) _____ by Your generous Spirit. Then (I) _____ will teach transgressors Your ways, and sinners shall be converted to You.

Deliver (me) _____ from the guilt of bloodshed, O God, the God of my salvation, and my tongue shall *sing aloud of Your righteousness. O Lord, open my lips, and my mouth shall show forth Your praise. For You do not desire sacrifice, or else I would give it; You do not delight in burnt offering. The sacrifices of God are a broken spirit, a broken and a contrite heart— these, O God, You will not despise. Amen.* *

*Psalm 51:1–17

BOUGHT WITH A PRICE

You and I were once bound in slavery to sin. But the Lord Jesus paid the price to set us free when He shed His blood at Calvary. That's what the Bible calls *redemption*. "In Him we have redemption through His blood, the forgiveness of sins, according to the riches of His grace" (Eph. 1:7). That's what Paul was referring to when he wrote: "You were bought at a price" (1 Cor. 6:20).

The blood of Jesus was not *spilled,* it was *shed.* It was no accident. The Lord chose to die in our place, shedding His precious blood on our behalf. Jesus said of Himself: "The Son of Man did not come to be served, but to serve, and to give His life a ransom for many" (Matt. 20:28).

Why did Christ redeem us? So "that the body of sin might be done away with, that we should no longer be slaves of sin" (Rom. 6:6). That is the only way we could "be dead indeed to sin, but alive to God in Christ Jesus our Lord" (Rom. 6:11).

We have been redeemed from sin, bondage and death. Recall your own personal redemption from sin. When did it happen? What was your heart condition at the time? What were the sins for which you needed God's redemption? How did you feel when you realized that because of the blood of Jesus, forgiveness had been applied to your life? **Describe (✍)** your experience of salvation on the lines below:

_____

_____

_____

Not only have you been redeemed from sin. You have been redeemed from death and hell. (See Revelation 1:18.) We have been set free to live abundant lives in Jesus Christ (John 10:10).

It's time to express your full gratitude to Jesus for the freedom from sin that He has given you through His shed blood. Many of the bondages of sin have been included in Paul's letter to the Galatians as "the works of the flesh": "Now the works of the flesh are evident, which are: adultery, fornication, uncleanness, lewdness, idolatry, sorcery, hatred, contentions, jealousies, outburst of wrath, selfish ambitions, dissensions, heresies, envy, murders, drunkenness, revelries, and the like" (Gal. 5:19–21). Using this list from Galatians, **check (✔)** all the bondages His shed blood has freed you from in your life.

❏ Adultery	❏ Contentions	❏ Envy
❏ Fornication	❏ Jealousies	❏ Murders
❏ Uncleanness	❏ Outbursts of wrath	❏ Drunkenness
❏ Lewdness		❏ Revelries
❏ Idolatry	❏ Selfish ambitions	❏ Other:
❏ Sorcery	❏ Dissensions	_____
❏ Hatred	❏ Heresies	_____

Now take a few minutes to pray, thanking Jesus for setting you free from sin, bondage and death.

Free! You have been set free. Every day we can rejoice—not only in what we have been redeemed from, but to what we have been redeemed. We have been set free from slavery to sin and satan. And we have been redeemed to a new liberty from sin and to a new life in Christ (2 Cor. 3:17–18).

What are we to do with the freedom bought by His blood? Listed below are a few of the ways believers can activate their new lives in Christ. Beside each item, **describe (✎)** how you are expressing your new life in Christ as a result of this wonderful freedom bought with the price of His shed blood.

Serving_____

Loving _____

Giving _____

Ministering to others _____

Ministering to God _____

Rejoicing _____

Worshiping _____

Witnessing _____

Other _____

Which of the above ways to express your new life in Christ have you not activated in your own life? Why not?

Tell somebody in sin and bondage that he or she can be set free. Share your testimony. Let God use your deliverance from sin to be a witness to someone else who needs deliverance and redemption.

Who needs to hear your testimony? Who do you know who is trapped in the bondage of sin and needs redemption from sin? **Write** down that person's name. Determine when you will share your testimony about the blood of Jesus and how you have been set free and write that date beside the person's name.

Name_____When? _____

Now **write** (✍) a prayer thanking Jesus for His shed blood that has set you free and asking Him to reveal the specific words that you can use to share your testimony with that person.

_____

_____

_____

_____

_____

_____

_____

REDEEMED TO . . .

Not only does the shed blood of Jesus Christ release us from sin, bondage and death; we are also redeemed to abundant life, freedom and eternal life.

When we have been redeemed by His blood, we can say: "I have been crucified with Christ; it is no longer I who live, but Christ lives in me; and the life which I now live in the flesh I live by faith in the Son of God, who loved me and gave Himself for me" (Gal. 2:20).

Yesterday we explored what we have been redeemed *from.* But the Bible is filled with the benefits of what you have been redeemed *to* in your new life in Christ. **Read** each passage listed below, and **describe** (✍) what you discover.

The Bible	The Benefit
John 3:16	_____
	_____
John 10:10	_____
	_____
Romans 10:9	_____
	_____
Romans 6:23	_____
	_____
1 John 2:25	_____
	_____

The Bible	The Benefit
Romans 15:13	_____
	_____
Philippians 1:9-11	_____
	_____
Galatians 5:22-23	_____
	_____

We have been filled with the fruit of the Spirit, with righteousness, with joy and abundant life through the redemption of Jesus' shed blood. Begin to praise Him! Lift your thanksgiving to Him in song, worship and prayer!

We have also been redeemed to liberty. His blood sets us free from legalism, religious bondage and stifling human traditions. In Mark 7:13, Jesus told the religious leaders of His day that they were "making the word of God of no effect through your tradition which you have handed down. And many such things you do."

Are there examples of legalism, religious bondages or stifling human traditions from which the blood of Jesus has set you free? On the lines below, **describe** (✍) those religious bondages from which you have been redeemed.

_____

_____

_____

We've also been redeemed to joy. From depression, doubt and discouragement, we have been filled with a supernatural joy that cannot be taken from us. Jesus speaks of that joy in the sixteenth chapter of John. **Read** John 16:16-33. Choose one of these verses that you can keep in your heart so your joy may be continually encouraged. **Write** (✍) this verse over the heart on the next page.

As a source of daily encouragement and strength, using an index card **make a list** of as many of the benefits of the blood of Christ and the anointing of the Holy Spirit as you can think of. Tape this card in a prominent spot in your home or carry it with you as a constant reminder when you leave the house. Remember: neither the world nor the devil can steal what the blood has redeemed!

Now pray, thanking Jesus for all the benefits of redemption His blood has bought for you both now and forever!

RECONCILED
BY THE BLOOD

In the story of the slave girl that I told at the beginning of chapter 11 in *The Blood*, who was in most need—the slave girl or the man who bought her? The slave girl, of course. In the same way, God did not need to be reconciled to man; man needed to be reconciled to God.

> For it pleased the Father that in Him all the fullness should dwell, and by Him to reconcile all things to Himself, by Him, whether things on earth or things in heaven, having made peace through the blood of His cross. And you, who once were alienated and enemies in your mind by wicked works, yet now He has reconciled in the body of His flesh through death, to present you holy, and blameless, and above reproach in His sight.
>
> —COLOSSIANS 1:19-22

In the Old Covenant, God instructed His people to offer sacrifices. These slain animals symbolically bore the punishment for sin that the people deserved. But the sacrifices had to be made over and over again. The Old Covenant was the shadow (Heb. 10:1). The New Covenant brought the reality. Christ died "once for all" (Heb. 10:10), atoning for our sins and bringing us back into fellowship with God. Righteousness demanded it; love offered it.

Now the Lord gives us a new responsibility: to share the message of reconciliation with the world.

> Now all things are of God, who has reconciled us to Himself through Jesus Christ, and has given us the ministry of reconciliation, that is, that God was in Christ reconciling the world to Himself, not imputing their trespasses to them, and has committed to us the word of reconciliation.
>
> —2 CORINTHIANS 5:18-19

How are you sharing the message of reconciliation with others in the world? Check (✔) the ways listed below that you are using to share the Good News with others. Circle (◯) the ways you would like to begin using to share the good news of reconciliation.

❑ Witnessing through an evangelism team at church

❑ Sharing the gospel with neighbors

❑ Telling those at work about Jesus

❑ Serving the "least of these" in Jesus' name

❑ Praying for the lost

❑ Other: _____

❑ Other: _____

In the time of Christ, Gentiles were excluded from the family of God because they were not part of the Old Covenant. They were known as "aliens from the commonwealth of Israel and strangers from the covenants of promise, having no hope and without God in the world" (Eph. 2:12).

But through the blood of the cross, these two groups—the Jews and the Gentiles—were made one, and Jesus "has broken down the middle wall of separation" (Eph. 2:14) so "that He might reconcile them both to God in one body through the cross, thereby putting to death the enmity" (Eph. 2:16). He made the Gentiles "fellow citizens with the saints and members of the household of God" (Eph. 2:19).

Removing the walls of hostility between people and between God and people is a part of Christ's great work as mediator of the New Covenant. That's a topic we will discuss in depth next week.

Below is a list of walls that keep us from sharing the gospel and from reconciling relationships with others. Prioritize the list of walls, from (1) the wall that keeps you from sharing the gospel most often to, (7) the wall that least affects you from sharing with others.

_____ Fear

_____ Rejection

_____ Feeling inadequate

_____ Prejudice

_____ Being too busy

_____ Lack of care for the lost

_____ Other: _____

Reconciliation through the blood of Christ begins with your relationship with Jesus. But it doesn't end there. It's not enough for you to be reconciled. You must take the good news to others.

Read the Great Commission of Jesus Christ. <u>Underline</u> what you are doing to fulfill that commission. **Circle (◯)** what you need to be doing.

The Great Commission

Jesus said, "All authority has been given to me in heaven and on earth. Go therefore and make disciples of all the nations, baptizing them in the name of the Father and of the Son and of the Holy Spirit, teaching them to observe all things that I have commanded you: and lo, I am with you always, even to the end of the age."

—MATTHEW 28:18–20

Now **write (✍)** a prayer, asking the Holy Spirit to empower you to fulfill this commission. Pray for the boldness and courage to share the good news of Jesus' reconciliation with others.

_____

_____

_____

JESUS, OUR MEDIATOR:
GRACE IN HIS BLOOD

I watched in amazement during the fall of 1993 as the state of Israel and the Palestinian Liberation Organization (PLO) signed an agreement that laid a framework for peace between people whose hostilities ran decades and centuries deep. Did those two powerful leaders just happen to meet one weekend? No. That historic moment came after years of negotiating through a third party—*a mediator.*

Because of His shed blood, the Lord Jesus has become our mediator with the Father. "And for this reason He is the Mediator of the new covenant, by means of death, for the redemption of the transgressions under the first covenant, that those who are called may receive the promise of the eternal inheritance" (Heb. 9:15).

Mankind has always needed a mediator. Under the Old Covenant, the high priest became the legal representative of the people regarding spiritual matters.

Today, Christ has become our High Priest through the shedding of His blood (Heb. 4:14). As our High Priest, He has the authority to be our legal mediator in heaven, representing us before the Father. Because of the cross "He is the Mediator of the new covenant, by means of death, for the redemption of the transgressions under the first covenant" (Heb. 9:15).

This week you will:

- Learn that Jesus is our High Priest and mediator through His shed blood.

- Discover there is nothing we can do to merit salvation.

- Realize that fearing God does not mean being afraid of Him.

- Recognize how God's hand guides us because of the shed blood of Jesus.

THIS WEEK'S OVERVIEW

DAY	STUDY TOPIC
ONE	Jesus, Our High Priest
TWO	There's Rest in the Blood
THREE	Fear and Faith
FOUR	Free Indeed
FIVE	The Father's Hand

It's my prayer that this week you will discover the amazing grace of God through the blood of Jesus. May any fears that you have of your loving Father be transformed into awe, respect and praise for all that He has done for you.

Memory Verse

As you study this week, learn and meditate on this scripture from Hebrews 10:19-22.

> Therefore, brethren, having boldness to enter the Holiest by the blood of Jesus, by a new and living way which He consecrated for us, through the veil, that is, His flesh, and having a High Priest over the house of God, let us draw near with a true heart in full assurance of faith, having our hearts sprinkled from an evil conscience and our bodies washed with pure water.

JESUS, OUR HIGH PRIEST

Christ has become our high priest through the shedding of His blood. That is what gives Him the authority to be our legal mediator in heaven, representing us before the Father. Because of the cross "He is the Mediator of the New Covenant, by means of death, for the redemption of the transgressions under the first covenant" (Heb. 9:15).

As our mediator, Christ intercedes on our behalf. The apostle Paul wrote, "It is Christ who died, and furthermore is also risen, who is even at the right hand of God, who also makes intercession for us" (Rom. 8:34). The Greek word for *intercession* is *entunchano,* which means "to meet with, to make petition."

Because He is our high priest, sin will not defeat us—no, not on a single score. He is our high priest, ever living to make intercession for us. "Therefore He is also able to save to the uttermost those who come to God through Him, since He always lives to make intercession for them" (Heb. 7:25).

When you approach the throne of God in prayer, how do you feel? With what attitude do you pray? **Circle (○)** the words that express your feelings and attitudes as you pray.

Nervous	Hopeful	Bold
Excited	Speechless	Condemned
Fearful	Loving	Other:
In awe	Helpless	_____

The primary attitude with which we come before God through the shed blood of Jesus should be boldness. The writer of Hebrews exhorted, "let us . . . come boldly to the throne of grace, that we may obtain mercy and find grace to help in time of need" (Heb. 4:16). Our wonderful Savior does not condemn us. He loves us. He died for us. "For there is one God and one Mediator between God and men, the Man Christ Jesus, who gave Himself a ransom for all" (1 Tim. 2:5-6).

Think about the following statements. Do you believe them to be true or false? **Indicate** your choice by putting a *T* on the line for each statement you believe to be true and an *F* for every statement you believe to be false.

____ 1. Because of my sin, I must approach God's throne in fear and trembling.

____ 2. Because I do not know how to pray properly, God will reject my prayers.

____ 3. Because I have unconfessed sin in my life, God's mercy is not available to me.

____ 4. As a punishment for my sin, God will condemn me.

____ 5. God will not hear my prayers because He is too busy with everybody else.

The answer to all of the above statements is false. Because of the shed blood of Jesus, you can approach God's throne boldly in prayer. The right words do not earn your entrance—His shed blood does! When you do not know how to pray, the Holy Spirit prays through you! God's mercy is based on what Jesus did on the cross—not your worthiness. Christ's forgiveness through His blood wipes away all condemnation. God hears each prayer you pray.

The password into God's throne room is: "I come by the blood." The moment you speak those words, entrance is yours.

Before the sacrifice of Christ, only the High Priest could enter into the holy of holies to meet with God. But Christ's redemptive plan swung open the door into the very presence of God. Because of the power of redemption that Jesus accomplished, we can enter the holy of holies.

> Therefore, brethren, having boldness to enter the Holiest by the blood of Jesus, by a new and living way which He consecrated for us, through the veil, that is, His flesh, and having a High Priest over the house of God, let us draw near with a true heart in full assurance of faith.
>
> —HEBREWS 10:19-22

These verses tell us that God has prepared four things for us.

1. The holiest, or most holy place—the place where God dwells
2. The blood of Jesus
3. A new and living way
4. A high priest

In response, we are to draw near with:

1. A true heart
2. Full assurance of faith
3. Hearts sprinkled from an evil conscience
4. Bodies washed with pure water

Look over these two lists from Hebrews 10 one more time. **Describe** (✍) the one thing about approaching the throne of God for which you are most thankful. _____

_____

_____

Why is that the item you chose? Praise Jesus for that one thing. Approach the throne of God boldly in Jesus' name through His shed blood. Pray boldly!

THERE'S REST
IN THE BLOOD

In 1975 I was ministering at a conference in Brockville, Ontario. A number of ministries were scheduled to take part in the conference. Among them was David du Plessis, a dynamic speaker known as "Mr. Pentecost." I had the privilege of meeting him for the first time while riding back to our hotel after a meeting. I hadn't been in the ministry long, and I was thrilled to have this opportunity to meet him face to face. David was a very dignified, quiet man and always carried his briefcase with him wherever he went. When we arrived at the hotel, he picked up his briefcase, got out of the car and made his way into the hotel. I quickly got out of the car and hurried after him.

In the elevator, moments later, I found myself alone with this great giant of the faith.

Very respectfully I said, "Mr. Pentecost (which is how he was known by many people), I want to ask you a question. I want to please God so badly. Please tell me—how can I please God?"

David didn't respond. He was very quiet. The elevator stopped, and we stepped out and started walking down the hall. Suddenly he stopped and stuck his finger in my chest, pushing me up against a wall. He looked at me with piercing eyes and said, "Don't even try. It's not your ability. It's His in you." I will never forget it as long as I live.

Then he said, "Good night," and picked up his briefcase and walked away while I stood there watching him. Later, he would become a very dear friend to me and a great influence on my life.

You may be struggling and agonizing over living the Christian life and trying to please God. You may feel as if you're getting nowhere. As Kathryn Kuhlman used to say, "Quit trying and surrender." That's all God asks you to do.

What are the areas in your life that are difficult to trust to God? If you are struggling in any of the areas listed below, describe (✎) the reason it is hard to trust God in that area. Circle (◯) the areas where you need to surrender and trust the blood of Jesus to bring healing to that situation.

My marriage _____

_____

My family_____

_____

My work _____

_____

My health _____

_____

My spiritual life_____

_____

My parents _____

_____

Other: _____

_____

Because of God's great mercy and love for us, "even when we were dead in trespasses, [He] made us alive together with Christ . . . and raised us up together, and made us sit together in the heavenly places in Christ Jesus" (Eph. 2:5-6).

Heaven will be ours, not because of what we have done, but because of "the exceeding riches of His grace in His kindness toward us in Christ Jesus" (Eph. 2:7). The blood of Christ covers our sin, and we receive forgiveness through faith because of the grace of God. It is a message that every believer needs to understand. We had nothing to do with earning our salvation. Religion says "Do." Jesus says, "Done!"

Now look at the area you circled above. Complete (✎) the following paragraph, using that area on the following blank lines.

> Because of the riches of God's kindness toward me, I commit _____ to the blood of Jesus Christ. I accept

His forgiveness for _____, and stand in faith through His grace for _____. I give _____ to God, and accept His answer to _____.

Pray this aloud.

Precious, Lord Jesus, I surrender all that I try to do to earn Your favor and grace. I accept the free gift of redemption through Your shed blood. Amen.

FEAR AND FAITH

Many Christians today have the wrong picture of God. From their childhood they have built an image of an almighty God who is harsh and austere—with glaring eyes of steel. They see Him with a whip in His hand, ready to beat them every time they make the slightest mistake. But God is nothing like that.

What kind of image did you have of God as you grew up? **Check (✔)** the words that best describe the image you had of God when you were a child.

❑   None

❑   A God to fear

❑   An angry and punishing God

❑   A loving and forgiving Father

❑   A distant and remote God

❑   A powerful God

❑   Other: _____

Though God occasionally chastises us for our good, He is always gentle, kind and loving to His children.

Read Psalm 103:6-13. **Describe (✍)** all the Father's qualities that this psalm mentions:

_____

_____

_____

Yes, we need to confess our sins to Christ and ask for forgiveness, but there is a great difference between coming before Him with fear and entering His presence with confidence.

Beneath our confession there needs to be a tremendous faith that what He did at Calvary was not for our judgment, but for our freedom. Stop looking at your failures and see God's mercy. He doesn't want to cast you aside but desires to hold you in His arms and say, "I love you."

Put an *x* on the line where you are right now.

I confess my failures.	I try to fix my failures.
I accept God's love and forgiveness.	I am afraid of God.
I know my past is forgiven.	I feel guilty about my past.

If you found yourself marking the right side of the lines, then step back and look once again at Calvary. Accept the fact that His shed blood completely washed your sins and failures away.

Let me share something with you that I learned from my father-in-law. He said, "Living the Christian life isn't difficult; it's impossible." It is impossible to obey the will of God with our own strength. But God sent His Holy Spirit to live in our hearts and empower us to obey His commands. God said through Ezekiel, "I will put My Spirit within you and cause you to walk in My statutes, and you will keep My judgments and do them" (Ezek. 36:27).

Say the following statement aloud:

> I have the power to live the Christian life, not through my own efforts but through the power of the Holy Spirit. I receive His power through the shed blood of Jesus Christ.

You have nothing to fear from God. He is not out to punish or judge you. He sent His Son to die for you, to shed His blood for you.

No longer do you live under the law—you live under grace.

If you have fears of God the Father, what are they? **Complete** (✎) these sentences:

1. God punishes when _____

   _____

2. God judges when _____

   _____

3. I am afraid to confess that _____

   _____

Now look over these sentences. Here's the good news: Jesus' blood has already been shed for what you have written. God is not angry with you. He wants you to run to Him and accept forgiveness through the blood of Jesus. Go back over these sentences. Thank Jesus for already dying for what you fear. Write a prayer of thanksgiving.

_____

_____

_____

Now **pray,** thanking Jesus for His amazing grace through His shed blood. Surrender your efforts to Him, and receive His grace!

FREE INDEED

Without the blood of Christ and God's grace it would be impossible for us to have victory over sin. Paul told what it's like to fight sin in the flesh. "For we know that the law is spiritual, but I am carnal, sold under sin" (Rom. 7:14). He added, "For I know that in me (that is, in my flesh) nothing good dwells; for to will is present with me, but how to perform what is good I do not find" (Rom. 7:18). Our flesh contains nothing that is good, and our righteousness is as filthy rags (Isa. 64:6). We can't make ourselves good enough to please God.

I remember praying, "Lord, there must be something I can do to please You."

He replied to me, "My greatest pleasure is when you allow Me to do the work."

I once heard a story about a Russian pastor who was thrown in prison by communist officials for preaching the gospel in the former Soviet Union. They did not allow this great saint of God to see another human being, and they fed him by pushing the food under the door. Years and years passed, and one day the Lord appeared to this man in prison. The man was so grateful to the Lord for coming to see him. He asked Him, "Is there anything I can give You to say thank You?"

"No, everything is Mine," the Lord responded. "There is nothing you can give Me."

"But, Lord, there must be something I can give You to say thank You."

"There is nothing you can give Me," the Lord repeated. "Your very body belongs to Me. Your very life is Mine."

But the man asked again, "Oh, please, there must be one thing I can give You.

Then the Lord said, "There is. Give Me your sins. That's all I want."

That is all He wants—our surrender. We turn our sins over to

Him because He is the only One who can subdue them. The Bible says: "Who is a God like You, pardoning iniquity and passing over the transgression of the remnant of His heritage? He does not retain His anger forever, because He delights in mercy. He will again have compassion on us, and will subdue our iniquities" (Mic. 7:18-19).

God delights in showing mercy. In your own words, **describe** (✍) the experience of mercy you received from the Lord, which pardoned your transgressions:

_____

_____

_____

_____

_____

_____

_____

_____

_____

_____

_____

_____

_____

_____

_____

_____

Read the Scriptures on the following page. **Describe** (✍) what each scripture says you have been set free from and what the scripture says you have been saved for.

The Bible	I'm Set Free From ... for ...
Romans 8:2-4	_____
	_____
John 8:32-36	_____
	_____
Romans 6:18	_____
	_____
Isaiah 61:1	_____
	_____
Galatians 5:1	_____
	_____

Think of your past bondages and sins. Think of all the bondages from which the blood has set you free. Now think of all you can do in Christ that you could not do before you were saved.

Write (✍) a prayer of thanksgiving for the liberty you have through the shed blood of Jesus Christ.

_____

_____

_____

THE FATHER'S HAND

My oldest daughter Jessica is now a beautiful young woman attending a university, but when she was just a toddler, I remember taking her for a walk in the woods. As we were about to walk up a little hill, I reached down and took hold of her hand. I didn't want her to slip and fall. Jessica's little hand was too weak to hold on to mine. She was depending on my strength to help her reach the top of the hill. Then the Holy Spirit said to me, "Who is holding your hand?"

As I thought about it, I said, "You are, Lord." How true it is. All of us are like my little girl Jessica. We're too weak to hold on to His hand. He holds on to our hands.

Check (✔) the times when you most need to hold on to God's hand:

❑ When you are afraid

❑ When you are doing the unfamiliar

❑ When you are lost

❑ When you are confused

❑ When you need direction and guidance

❑ When you don't know how to pray

❑ When you are in danger of failing or falling

❑ When:_____

The Bible says, "For I, the Lord your God, will hold your right hand, saying to you, 'Fear not, I will help you' " (Isa. 41:13). The Old Covenant promised it, and so did the New. Jesus said, "And I give them eternal life, and they shall never perish; neither shall anyone snatch them out of My hand" (John 10:28).

The first time I read that Scripture passage I said, "Thank You,

Lord, for reaching down and holding me." Several years later, I was studying the passage again, and I began to praise the Lord as I noticed what the next verse said. "My Father, who has given them to Me, is greater than all; and no one is able to snatch them out of My Father's hand" (John 10:29).

Below is the drawing of a hand representing the hand of God. Over that hand, **write** (✍) the names of all those things and persons you need to place in His hand.

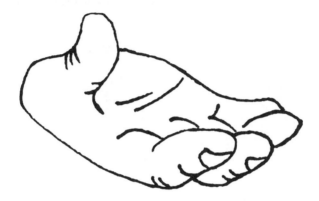

Now **write** (✍) a prayer completely surrendering each thing that you have written into the hand of God.

_____

_____

_____

_____

Not only is Jesus holding my hand, but the Father is holding it, too. When He reaches out to you, you can be sure that He will never let go. The only time Jesus will let you go is when you push Him away.

Tell Jesus right now that you will not push Him away, ever!

The Master's touch is so important in our lives. His hand delivers us from every bondage in life. Remember, His shed blood flowed through His hands for us. There are many scriptures that talk about God's hands and His touch. **Read** Psalm 37:23-24; Isaiah 41:13; and John 10:29. Then **describe** (✍) what a touch from God means to you.

To me, His touch means . . .

_____

_____

_____

Pray that the Master will touch you now with His nail-scarred hands, covering you with His blood, which cleanses, forgives and heals.

WEEK SEVEN

GOD'S GRACE AND YOUR NEW FAMILY

One evening I was watching a Christian television program. A preacher was teaching about grace. He caught my attention when he said, "Let me tell you what grace really is. Let's suppose that a man has an only child who is murdered. The man has three choices. He can kill the man for murdering his son, which would be revenge. He can let the law deal with him, which would be justice. Or he can forgive him, adopt him and give him his son's place. Now that's grace."

That is exactly what God did when He saved you and me. We were the ones who put His Son on the cross. It was for our sins and iniquities that Jesus shed His precious blood. And because of His sacrificial death, when we repent of our sins and accept Jesus as Savior and Lord, God forgives us. Not only that, but we have been adopted into God's wonderful family. "Behold what manner of love the Father has bestowed on us, that we should be called children of God!" (1 John 3:1).

How true are the words of the song:

> Amazing grace! how sweet the sound,
> That saved a wretch like me!
> I once was lost, but now am found,
> Was blind, but now I see.

So great is the Father's grace that Jesus said, "You . . . have loved them as You have loved Me" (John 17:23). And so great is His love that Psalm 139:17-18 says: "How precious also are Your thoughts to me, O God! How great is the sum of them! If I should count them, they would be more in number than the sand. When I awake, I am still with You."

Not only does He love us, but He thinks about us all the time. The Bible says that God will never forget us. As you study this week, you will:

- Find out about your new family in Christ.
- Understand the choice of faith confronting you.
- Discover how you have been sealed by the Holy Spirit.
- Uncover the power of forgiveness.
- Realize the tremendous power of grace.

THIS WEEK'S OVERVIEW	
DAY	STUDY TOPIC
ONE	Graven on His Palms
TWO	A Matter of Choice
THREE	The Great Seal
FOUR	Seventy Times Seven
FIVE	The Power of Grace

You need to accept the grace and power from Jesus Christ made available to you through His blood. This is your week for doing just that! Get ready to be blessed!

I encourage you to read each scripture, do each exercise, spend significant time with God in prayer and claim the power of the blood each day.

Memory Verse

As you study and pray this week, meditate on the grace and power of Christ. Get the following Word from God into your spirit man:

Yes, I have loved you with an everlasting love;
Therefore with lovingkindness I have drawn you.

—JEREMIAH 31:3

Through the Lord's mercies we are not consumed,
Because His compassions fail not.
They are new every morning;
Great is Your faithfulness.

—LAMENTATIONS 3:22–23

DAY 1

GRAVEN ON
HIS PALMS

The words of Isaiah 49:15-16 express the Lord's heart toward us: "Can a woman forget her nursing child, and not have compassion on the son of her womb? Surely they may forget, yet I will not forget you. See, I have inscribed you on the palms of My hands."

Throughout eternity, Christ's nail prints are an everlasting reminder of His great love for you and me.

Unfortunately, some do not know His love. They accept Him to escape hell. They accept Him on the basis of fear. They are looking for a fire escape. Those who receive Him on the basis of fear are always attempting to do something to prove they are really saved. But their fear results in futile legalism and useless works.

On the other hand, the person who accepts Christ on the basis of love discovers, "It is not what I have done, but what He has done for me." They see how loving He is.

When you see His love, you will not see defeat. When you see heaven, you won't see hell. When you see mercy, you won't see judgment.

Most people have been in the courtroom too long. Every time they come before the Lord, they see themselves appearing before a condemning judge. But the Word says: "Most assuredly, I say to you, he who hears My word and believes in Him who sent Me has everlasting life, and shall not come into judgment, but has passed from death into life" (John 5:24).

When Jesus hung on the cross, your sentence of death was waived. The Father took His judicial robe off, put down the gavel and said, "Come into the family room. Come home!" Instead of presiding over a court of justice, I see Him standing in the family room, waiting for His children to return.

When you repent and accept God's grace, He adopts you into His family. God did not receive you so that He could "unadopt" and disinherit you later. He does not threaten to throw you out of the family.

The Lord brings us in and *keeps* us in.

Answer the following questions, **circling** (◯) the answer which best describes your response.

1. When I pray, God loves me:
    More   **The same**   Less

2. When I read my Bible, God loves me:
    More   **The same**   Less

3. When I do right things, God loves me:
    More   **The same**   Less

God will never love you more or less than He loves you right now or than He loved you when Jesus shed His blood for you. In other words, His love is not conditional. His love is unchanging, constant and eternal.

Describe (✍) what each of the following scriptures say about God's love:

Jeremiah 31:3 _____

_____

_____

Lamentations 3:22–23 _____

_____

_____

1 John 4:8 _____

_____

_____

Read 1 Corinthians 13, which not only describes the qualities of God's love for us, but also what our love for others needs to be.

Are you experiencing God's love in your life? Have you shown "God-like" love to others? Beside each quality of God's love listed below, **describe** (✍) how you can show that love in a specific way to someone else.

God's love . . .	I can show this quality of God's love by . . .
is patient	_____
is kind	_____
does not envy	_____
is not proud	_____
does not seek its own	_____
is not easily provoked	_____
thinks no evil	_____
does not rejoice in iniquity	_____
rejoices in truth	_____
bears all things	_____
believes all things	_____
hopes all things	_____
endures all things	_____
never fails	_____

In which of the above areas are you having difficulty experiencing God's love? **Circle** (◯) those areas. Now **underline** the areas where you have difficulty expressing God's love to someone else. Consider how you can experience more of God's love in and through your life.

As you pray today, thank God for His infinite love for you, which He manifested in the shed blood of Jesus Christ.

DAY 2

A MATTER OF CHOICE

A man once asked me, "If God does everything, how is choice involved?" It was a valid question. "Before you were saved, did you seek the Lord, or did He seek you?" I asked him.

"He sought me," he replied.

"Did you produce the faith to believe? Or did He give it to you?"

"He gave it to me."

"Well, if God did all of those things then, who is keeping you now? Are you keeping yourself? And who will take you into heaven? Can you do it yourself?" I asked. Finally I said, "You have nothing to do with it."

"All that is good," he responded, "but where is choice?"

"All you need to say is yes to Jesus, and these things will be yours. Your choice is just to accept what He has done for you."

A big smile broke across his face. "I see it!"

Jesus told His disciples, "You did not choose Me, but I chose you and appointed you" (John 15:16). Have you made that free choice to accept the shed blood of Jesus for your salvation?

❑ Yes

❑ No

If you checked "yes," then take a moment to praise and thank Jesus for your salvation. If you checked "no," then will you pray this prayer aloud right now?

> *Lord Jesus, I make the choice to receive the gift of grace bought by Your blood on the cross. I repent of my sin. Cleanse and purify me by Your shed blood. I surrender to You as my Lord and Savior. Thank You for saving me and giving me the gift of Your Holy Spirit. Amen.*

That's the most important choice you will ever make in life.

Don't take it lightly. Scripture warns us that God's grace must never be misused. "We then, as workers together with Him also plead with you not to receive the grace of God in vain" (2 Cor. 6:1). Salvation is ours because of what the Lord has done, not because of our perfection. What produces failure? It is when we stop trusting God and start relying on ourselves. The prophet Ezekiel said: "When I say to the righteous that he shall surely live, but he trusts in his own righteousness and commits iniquity, none of his righteous works shall be remembered; but because of the iniquity that he has committed, he shall die" (Ezek. 33:13).

I believe that we are secure in our salvation, but we can risk losing what He has given us. For Peter said: "For if, after they have escaped the pollutions of the world through the knowledge of the Lord and Savior Jesus Christ, they are again entangled in them and overcome, the latter end is worse for them than the beginning. For it would have been better for them not to have known the way of righteousness, than having known it, to turn from the holy commandment delivered to them" (2 Pet. 2:20–21).

Where is the balance? God chooses us but always gives us the choice to respond. If someone came to me with a gun pointed at my head and said, "Deny Christ or die," I would say, "Shoot." Why? Because my commitment to Christ is not temporary; it's eternal.

When I met the Lord it was not a "goose-bump," momentary experience. At that moment I became a totally new person. It was an instantaneous new birth. It is a continuous salvation.

What should be our response to the Lord in return for His eternal benefits? The psalmist said: "I will take up the cup of salvation, and call upon the name of the Lord" (Ps. 116:13). **Read** Psalm 116. **Describe (✐)** how the psalmist responded to the Lord's salvation:

_____

_____

_____

This salvation is even better than we can think. We can have complete confidence that He will finish what He has started . . . that He has committed to keep us. (See Philippians 1:6.) But how can we know that in our hearts? We shall study that together tomorrow.

What response will you make to the Lord for His eternal benefits? **Underline** your responses:

Praise

Thanksgiving

Rejoicing

Love

Telling others

Obedience

Other: _____

Now **pray**, confessing these responses to the Lord for His wonderful salvation.

THE GREAT SEAL

When we are washed by His blood and cleansed by the Word, then the Lord puts the seal of the Holy Spirit on us. Paul wrote: "In Him you also trusted, after you heard the word of truth, the gospel of your salvation; in whom also, having believed, you were sealed with the Holy Spirit of promise, who is the guarantee of our inheritance until the redemption of the purchased possession, to the praise of His glory" (Eph. 1:13-14).

When you hear the word *seal,* what images and thoughts come to your mind? List (✍) a few of those images here:

_____

_____

_____

A seal is a symbol of protection. It says, "This is mine. Put it aside, and leave it for me. No one is to touch it because I am coming back to claim it." The Lord does not seal anything that He does not plan to redeem. And He would not build mansions unless He was waiting for us to come home (John 14:2-3). We will remain sealed until Christ takes us home "to an inheritance incorruptible and undefiled and that does not fade away, reserved in heaven for you" (1 Pet. 1:4).

The inheritance is for those "who are kept by the power of God through faith for salvation ready to be revealed in the last time" (1 Pet. 1:5). Scripture reveals many things about our eternal inheritance. Look up the promises on the following page about your inheritance and describe (✍) each one.

Bible Promise	My inheritance is . . .
Psalm 16:5	_____
	_____
Psalm 37:18	_____
	_____
Ephesians 1:11-14	_____
	_____
Ephesians 1:18-19	_____
	_____
Colossians 1:13-15	_____
	_____
Hebrews 9:15	_____
	_____
1 Peter 1:3-5	_____
	_____

The seal on us for our inheritance will not be removed until His final work has been completed. Paul said that we "who have the firstfruits of the Spirit, even we ourselves groan within ourselves, eagerly waiting for the adoption, the redemption of our body" (Rom. 8:23). The work is complete when the final trumpet sounds.

> The dead will be raised incorruptible, and we shall be changed. For this corruptible must put on incorruption, and this mortal must put on immortality. So when this corruptible has put on incorruption, and this mortal has put on immortality, then shall be brought to pass the saying that is written: "Death is swallowed up in victory."
>
> —1 CORINTHIANS 15:52-54

The Holy Spirit has sealed you for an eternal inheritance through the shed blood of Jesus Christ. Whom do you know that needs to be sealed by His Spirit? Below is a representation of the Holy Spirit as a dove (Matt. 3:16). Over the dove, **write (✍)** the name of each person for whom you will begin praying who needs to confess Jesus as Lord and Savior and be sealed by His Spirit.

Now **pray** for each of these persons by name. You may wish to pray these words:

> *Lord Jesus, I pray for* _____ *(names),*
> *that Your precious Holy Spirit would convict them and*
> *lead them to repentance and salvation through Your*
> *blood that they might be sealed unto Your eternal*
> *inheritance. Amen.*

DAY 4

SEVENTY TIMES SEVEN

As long as you accept what Christ's blood has done for you, no power on earth can break God's seal (2 Tim. 1:12). "For I am persuaded that neither death nor life, nor angels nor principalities nor powers, nor things present nor things to come, nor height nor depth, nor any other created thing, shall be able to separate us from the love of God which is in Christ Jesus our Lord" (Rom. 8:38-39).

You may ask, "Are you telling me that God loves me in spite of myself?" Yes. Regardless of our inconsistencies, He still loves us. He adopted us even though we were responsible for the death of His Son. And He welcomes us back even when we falter and fail.

Is there an area of your life in which you continually falter and fail? Don't delay in confessing that to the Lord. Don't hold on to your failures and sins. **Take some time right now and pray and ask the Lord to reveal any areas in your life of which you may be unaware but are areas that you need to confess to Him in prayer.**

Ask immediately for His forgiveness through Jesus' blood.

Some people worry, *What if I make the same mistake again and again? Will He still pardon me?* Peter asked Jesus the same question. "'Lord, how often shall my brother sin against me, and I forgive him? Up to seven times?' Jesus said to him, 'I do not say to you, up to seven times, but up to seventy times seven'" (Matt. 18:21-22).

The Lord's answer does not mean Christians can live in sin without repenting and still make heaven. Far from it. Those who abuse the forgiving nature of God have never experienced His true salvation. What God offers is more than eternal security—He gives us eternal grace.

Remember these steps in dealing with habitual sin in your life.

- Admit it.
- Quit it.
- Forget it.

Is there habitual sin in your life that the power of His Spirit needs to break right now? **Complete (✍)** each of the following sentences.

I admit _____.

I will quit _____.

I can now forget _____.

It is God's transforming grace that makes redemption possible and prepares us to live godly lives. "For the grace of God that brings salvation has appeared to all men, teaching us that, denying ungodliness and worldly lusts, we should live soberly, righteously, and godly in the present age, looking for the blessed hope and glorious appearing of our great God and Savior Jesus Christ, who gave Himself for us, that He might redeem us from every lawless deed and purify for Himself His own special people, zealous for good works" (Titus 2:11-14).

How would you **define** grace?

_____

_____

_____

_____

The Greek definition of *grace* includes both "free gift" and "joy." That's right. His grace is something you can't earn and something that brings you joy. **Describe (✍)** the effect of God's grace in your life.

I rejoice because His grace in my life has . . .

_____

_____

_____

_____

When you come face to face with the saving grace of God, it will bring a hunger for righteousness and godliness. Because of the finished work of Calvary, God sent His Holy Spirit to provide strength to live holy lives. Paul said that we "do not live according to the sinful nature but according to the Spirit" (Rom. 8:4, NIV).

What God said to the prophet Zechariah is still true: "'Not by might nor by power, but by My Spirit' says the LORD of hosts" (Zech. 4:6).

You may be facing temptation that seems like a mountain that will crush you. But because of the Spirit of the Lord and because of His grace, you can take that mountain apart stone by stone.

Describe (✍) a temptation that you are facing right now.

_____

_____

_____

_____

Pray right now, claiming the power of His forgiveness to conquer every temptation.

THE POWER OF GRACE

With God's grace comes great power. "With great power the apostles gave witness to the resurrection of the Lord Jesus. And great grace was upon them all" (Acts 4:33). In the Book of Acts we see what the power of God accomplished in the first Christians. After each listed evidence of the power of the Holy Spirit, **complete** (✍) the sentence.

- *They received power and became witnesses.* "But you shall receive power when the Holy Spirit has come upon you; and you shall be witnesses to Me" (Acts 1:8).

  An evidence of the Spirit's power in me is _____

  _____.

- *The Holy Spirit changed their speech.* They began speaking in unknown tongues (Acts 2:4) and speaking God's Word with boldness (Acts 4:31).

  I see His boldness in my life through _____

  _____.

- *Their demeanor was changed.* Stephen was the most dramatic example of this. When the Holy Spirit came upon Stephen while he was on trial, "all who sat in the council, looking steadfastly at him, saw his face as the face of an angel" (Acts 6:15).

  With the Spirit's power, my demeanor has changed in this way: _____

  _____.

I believe that when God's anointing is on someone, the presence of the Holy Spirit is evident to those around that person. There is a look of divine power and joy on his or her face, a sense of authority in the person's voice. That's why Peter and John told the lame man, "Look at us" (Acts 3:4). When that lame man looked at them, they knew he would be able to see that the power of God was upon them.

- *The Holy Spirit gave them boldness.* "Now when they saw the boldness of Peter and John, and perceived that they were uneducated and untrained men, they marveled" (Acts 4:13). They had no more fear, but glorious boldness to proclaim the good news of the gospel.

The Holy Spirit makes me bold to_____

_____.

- *The Holy Spirit changed their relationships.* Peter said that he was a witness of what Jesus had done, "and so also is the Holy Spirit" (Acts 5:32). Here we see the Holy Spirit as their companion and helper.

The Holy Spirit has changed my relationships by _____

_____.

- *The Holy Spirit changed their position.* Stephen started out in the church as one who served others (Acts 6:5), but he ended up being a mighty evangelist (Acts 6:8-10).

The position the Holy Spirit has given me is _____

_____.

- *The Holy Spirit changed their vision.* "But he, being full of the Holy Spirit, gazed into heaven and saw the glory of God, and Jesus standing at the right hand of God" (Acts 7:55).

The vision the Holy Spirit is giving me is _____

_____.

The Holy Spirit's great power is available to us today because we have also received God's "great grace" (Acts 4:33).

The Holy Spirit in our lives is a reminder that Christ has bled and died, risen again and ascended to the right hand of His Father.

Write (✍) a prayer thanking Jesus for giving you His Holy Spirit of grace through His shed blood.

_____

_____

_____

WEEK EIGHT

COMMUNION IN
THE COMMUNION

A few years ago I held a crusade where more than twelve thousand people jammed a stadium at a fairgrounds to hear the Word of God preached. As I ministered on the platform, my eyes were drawn to a group of Roman Catholic nuns dressed in distinctive ankle-length habits sitting near the front in the massive crowd. Because I was taught by Catholic nuns when I was a boy, I have a special place in my heart for them. At one point in the service I called them up onto the platform—forty-nine in all. We talked, and I discovered they were Catholic Charismatics who had driven six hours to attend the service.

Before they returned to their seats, I invited them to join me in leading the people in a verse of "How Great Thou Art." Just before the closing line of the song, the Catholic nuns did something I will never forget. With spontaneous choreographed perfection, each of the forty-nine Catholic nuns produced a wooden cross from her habit and raised it heavenwards. They all sang the final chorus, "How great Thou art, how great Thou art!" It was a very powerful moment in the service.

After the service I had a little more time to talk with them. I learned they belonged to an order that was founded by their mother general, a tall woman with piercing blue eyes. (I found out later that a mother general is even higher than a mother superior.)

"Why don't you come and visit our convent?" the mother general asked me.

"I would love to come," I told her. A few months later I did. The convent was located on rolling hills in a river valley. The sisters built all of the buildings, including a retreat center and a farm where they raise their own food.

The sisters served a beautiful turkey dinner, complete with vegetables they had grown themselves, to me and a few friends who had accompanied me. After dinner they asked, "Would you mind if we served you communion?"

"Not at all. I would love it," I said. (Apparently they felt it would be permissible to serve me because I had been baptized in the Greek Orthodox church as a child.)

I didn't realize the Lord had something in store for me that night that would impact my life greatly. All forty-nine nuns, along with my friends and me, went to the newly built prayer chapel. The nuns began worshiping the Lord, singing in the Spirit and blessing the Lord for about half an hour. The sisters gave several words of prophecy that encouraged me.

By then I was on my knees crying because I sensed such a tremendous presence of the Lord there. It was an anointing that I had never before experienced in a communion service, not even in my own church. It was a divine, powerful presence of God that I can't describe except to say, "Jesus walked into that little room."

THIS WEEK'S OVERVIEW

DAY	STUDY TOPIC
ONE	Communion With Jesus
TWO	Being Worthy
THREE	What Do We Remember?
FOUR	Come Into the Throne Room
FIVE	There's Power in the Blood

This week you will:

- Discover how to commune with Jesus through remembering His shed blood in communion.

- Understand how to partake of the Lord's Supper "worthily."

- Gain insight into what we actually remember in the Lord's supper.

- Be ushered into the throne room of God.

Memory Verse

As you study and pray this week, I invite you to memorize this important verse about communion from the Word.

And when He had given thanks, He broke it and said, "Take, eat; this is My body which is broken for you; do this in remembrance of Me." In the same manner He also took the cup after supper, saying, "This cup is the New Covenant in My blood. This do, as often as you drink it, in remembrance of me." For as often as you eat this bread and drink this cup, you proclaim the Lord's death until He comes.

—1 CORINTHIANS 11:23-26

COMMUNION WITH JESUS

Remember my sharing about the communion invitation from the Catholic sisters? Well, just as they were finishing a time of worship in that communion service, I began to feel a numbness in my arms and chest. I didn't know that the mother general had just gone to the table and picked up the communion wafer. She began to speak the words of the apostle Paul from 1 Corinthians 11: "For I received from the Lord that which I also delivered to you: that the Lord Jesus on the same night in which He was betrayed took bread" (v. 23).

Communion is a very special time of fellowship for the believer. On the lines below, briefly **describe** (✍) the most memorable time of communion you have experienced.

_____

_____

_____

One of my most memorable times of communion was with those nuns. As I was kneeling and praising the Lord with my hands extended directly in front of me, the mother general put the wafer in my mouth.

At that moment I felt a fire literally go through me, and as that took place something else amazing happened. I sensed on the tips of my fingers something like a robe—a soft, silky fabric. I thought maybe I was touching one of the sister's robes or that my mind was playing tricks on me. I wasn't sure what it was. So I opened my eyes to see whether someone had stepped in front of me. There was no one.

I wanted to make sure it wasn't just my mind, so I closed my eyes again. By this time I was weeping and basking in the presence of God that filled the room. Again I felt the robe. I thought,

This can't be. I opened my eyes. As before, nothing was there.

I closed my eyes again, and as quickly as I did, I felt the same thing again—some type of soft, flowing fabric. I paused for a moment and I moved my hands closer toward each other. Then I stopped for I could not move them any closer. Something was there in front of me. It felt what seemed like a person's body. The experience I had that evening as I knelt there in prayer was unlike anything I had ever known. It was as if I was kneeling at the feet of Jesus.

After that communion service, I couldn't quit singing. That entire night I felt as if I were floating. I went back to my hotel room and asked the Lord, "What happened to me?" The Lord began to open my understanding about the subject of communion.

Whenever we have communion, we are having communion with the Lord. When we celebrate the Lord's supper, He is there.

Describe (✍) the thoughts that you have had as you commune with Jesus through the sacrament of communion.

When I partake of the bread, I _____

_____.

When I take the cup, I _____

_____.

I want to share with you what the Lord showed me through that experience and as I studied the Word. In 1 Corinthians 10:16, the Bible says: "The cup of blessing which we bless, is it not the communion of the blood of Christ? The bread which we break, is it not the communion of the body of Christ?"

This verse says, "There is communion in the communion." Often when we take communion, we don't realize that we are to have communion with the Lord Himself. It's not just a practice because of tradition or what we were told by our fathers or our mothers. Yes, it's a remembrance of what He did for us two thousand years ago at Calvary. But at the same time, it is a communion with Him in the present! He comes today to fellowship with you as your son or daughter or loved one would.

Each of the verses on the following page tell us something about the Lord's Supper. **Read** each of the verses and **describe** (✍) what that verse says to you about your communion with the living Christ.

Matthew 26:26-29   _____

_____

Luke 22:14-22   _____

_____

John 6:53-58   _____

_____

1 Corinthians 10:16-17 _____

_____

During your prayer time today **thank** Jesus for His broken body and shed blood.

BEING WORTHY

I was so thrilled by this new understanding about the Lord's Supper that I wanted to do everything I could to keep the "communion within communion." Paul's warning in 1 Corinthians 11:27 became so real: "Therefore whoever eats this bread or drinks this cup of the Lord in an unworthy manner will be guilty of the body and blood of the Lord."

Why was he saying this to the Corinthian church? What would cause them to turn communion with the Lord into a vain ceremony? The apostle Paul gives us five reasons.

1. There were divisions among them (v. 18).
2. There were heretical teachings in the church (v. 19).
3. Paul recognized selfishness in this church (v. 21).
4. The people had lost all respect for the house of God (v. 22).
5. They were very proud and looked down on people outside the church (v. 22).

Using this checklist, **rate** your own church. If any of the following symptoms apply to your congregation, **check (✔)** the box beside that symptom:

❑   Divisions or a divisive spirit

❑   Heretical or compromised teachings about the Word

❑   Selfishness among the members or leadership

❑   Lack of respect for or despising of the house of God

❑   Pride among the members of the church

❑   People who look down on others or are self-righteous

When Paul warned against celebrating the Lord's supper in an unworthy manner, he was talking about the sins in the Corinthian church. Some of their sins were even committed at the Lord's table! Paul said that many of the Corinthians were "weak and sick," and some had even died because of their lack of discernment. That's a negative thing. But by the same token, if we partake worthily, I believe there will be health and strength rather than weakness and sickness.

Paul goes on to say: "For if we would judge ourselves, we would not be judged. But when we are judged, we are chastened by the Lord, that we may not be condemned with the world" (vv. 31-32). If we would judge ourselves, then God wouldn't have to judge us. But if He does judge, He is only doing it for the sake of our redemption.

In Psalm 32 we see both kinds of judgment—how God judges man; and how man can judge himself. When David did not judge himself and confess his sin rather keeping silent, he describes what took place: "When I kept silent, my bones grew old, through my groaning all the day long" (v. 3). His physical body was affected. Remember that Paul said, "For this reason [participating in communion unworthily] many are weak and sick among you" (1 Cor. 11:30).

God often judges us by withdrawing a sense of His presence from us. Living without the presence of the Lord is like the dryness of a summer without rain. "For day and night Your hand was heavy upon me; my vitality was turned into the drought of summer" (Ps. 32:4).

How would you describe your own times of communion with the Lord recently? Are they fresh and alive? Or would you, like David, describe a "drought" in your fellowship with the Lord? On each line below, **put an x** where your relationship has been.

Alive	Dying
Fresh	Stale
Dynamic	Powerless

If your marks were on the right side of the lines, then your relationship with the Lord may need help and healing. David demonstrated the way to come back into the Lord's favor when he stated: "I acknowledged my sin to You, and my iniquity I have not hidden. I said, 'I will confess my transgressions to the Lord,' and You forgave the iniquity of my sin" (Ps. 32:5).

The book of 1 John supports David's actions when it tells us: "If we confess our sins, He is faithful and just to forgive us our sins and to cleanse us from all unrighteousness" (1 John 1:9). God always forgives us when we confess. If anything is blocking your communion with the Lord now, **confess** it and come to His table ready to commune with Him.

WHAT DO
WE REMEMBER?

W hen Jesus was celebrating the first communion with His disciples, He told them, "Do this in remembrance of Me" (Luke 22:19). What should we remember when we come to the Lord's table?

First, dear saint, I know you thank God that Jesus died in your place to free you from the consequences of your sins. But He did so many other things for you on the cross. The fifty-third chapter of Isaiah speaks prophetically of many of the things that Jesus' death on the cross would accomplish in the life of the believer. **Read** this chapter. On the lines below **describe** (✎) the benefits Isaiah listed as a result of Jesus' sacrifice.

The Scriptures are clear: Jesus not only died to take away our sins, He died to take away our sicknesses. It's important to God that we remember what He has done for us—that's why we celebrate the Lord's supper.

I believe the psalmist was also speaking prophetically of the benefits of the cross when he wrote Psalm 103. "Bless the LORD, O my soul, and forget not all His benefits" (v. 2). When we forget what God has done for us, He is grieved. **Complete** (✎) the following sentences, describing the benefits shown in Psalm 103.

- "Who forgives all your iniquities" (v. 3). All your sins are washed away; all your sins are forgiven. All you have to do is repent and receive Him as your Savior.

The sin for which I am most thankful Jesus forgave me was:

_____

- "Who heals all your diseases" (v. 3). I'm so glad the verse doesn't say, "Who forgave" and "who healed." It says, "Who forgives" (present tense) and "who heals" (present tense). He *still* forgives; He *still* heals.

What disease has He healed in your life?

_____

- "Who redeems your life from destruction" (v. 4).

How has the Lord saved you from physical harm?

_____

- "Who crowns you with lovingkindness and tender mercies" (v. 4).

What kindness have you most recently experienced from the Lord?

_____

- "Who satisfies your mouth with good things" (v. 5). The Bible says God satisfies you with good things. He never gives bad things; He always gives good things. As my friend Oral Roberts says, "God is a good God."

What good things have you recently received from the Lord?

_____

- "So that your youth is renewed like the eagle's" (v. 5). When we know His benefits, He'll renew us.

How have you been renewed by the Lord?

_____

- "The Lord executes righteousness and justice for all who are oppressed" (v. 6). Because of the cross, we are defended from the oppressor.

From what oppression or oppressor has He delivered you?

_____

As you pray today, **thank** our wonderful Lord for all His mighty benefits that He has provided for you through the shed blood of Jesus Christ.

COME INTO THE
THRONE ROOM

I n Philippians 2:5–8, Paul shares the seven "steps" Jesus took to descend from His heavenly throne to the cross.

As I share with you these seven steps, consider your own walk with God. How can these steps become real in your daily life? Answer (✐) the question after the description of each step.

1. "Who, being in the form of God, did not consider it robbery to be equal with God" (v. 6)

    What daily action can you take to avoid "playing God" in your own life?

    _____

2. "But made Himself of no reputation" (v. 7)

    Describe the reputation you have as a follower of Jesus Christ.

    _____

3. "Taking the form of a bondservant" (v. 7)

    How will you be a servant to Jesus?

    _____

4. "And coming in the likeness of men" (v. 7)

    How are you being transformed into His likeness?

    _____

5. "And being found in appearance as a man" (v. 8)

How does the Holy Spirit manifest Himself in you?

_____

6. "He humbled Himself" (v. 8)

In what or whom do you take pride?

_____

7. "And became obedient to the point of death, even the death of the cross" (v. 8)

Under what circumstances would you die for Jesus?

_____

But God also took seven "steps" to restore Christ's throne to Him. We read these steps in Philippians 2:9-11.

1. "Therefore God also has highly exalted Him" (v. 9)
2. "And given Him the name which is above every name" (v. 9)
3. "That at the name of Jesus every knee should bow" (v. 10)
4. "Of those in heaven" (v. 10).
5. "And of those on earth" (v. 10).
6. "And of those under the earth" (v. 10).
7. "And that every tongue should confess that Jesus Christ is Lord, to the glory of God the Father" (v. 11)

<u>Underline</u> the step above for which you want to give God praise. In the Book of Hebrews the scripture declares that after the Lord Jesus purged our sins, He "sat down at the right hand of the Majesty on high" (Heb. 1:3). Sitting speaks of a finished work; the right hand speaks of power. Jesus received all authority and all power. "Majesty on high" speaks of Jesus as the King of kings and Lord of lords.

Because He is on that throne, the Bible says we have "boldness to enter the Holiest by the blood of Jesus" (Heb. 10:19). Jesus went from the throne to the cross to save us. He went from the cross to the throne to become our high priest and enable us to enter God's presence.

Whenever you celebrate the Lord's supper, remember that it is because of the blood of Jesus Christ that we can have fellowship with God. And as we recall what He has done for us when His body was broken and His blood was shed, then the presence of God will descend.

I've seen in my own experience that through the blood of Jesus, the anointing of God always comes—not only on my private, personal prayer life, but even during church services and the great miracle services.

I never conduct a service without thanking Him for the blood. For I have discovered that where the blood is honored, the presence of God descends and miracles take place. In the Old Covenant, God responded with fire when blood was offered on the altar. So it is today. When the blood of Jesus is honored, when the cross is honored, the Holy Spirit comes and touches people's lives.

I pray that the presence of the Holy Spirit will increase and become great in your life as a result of reading this study guide. And I pray your love for the Lord will be enlarged until that glorious day when you see Him face to face.

Write (✍) a prayer thanking Jesus for His shed blood.

_____

_____

_____

_____

_____

_____

THERE'S POWER
IN THE BLOOD

This last study is an opportunity for you to reflect upon what you have learned about the blood of Jesus during this study. Isn't it wonderful to learn about and apply the blood of Jesus? **Complete (✑)** these sentences:

• Some promises made through the blood covenant are:

_____

_____

_____

• My favorite scripture about the blood is:

_____

_____

_____

• I apply the blood to:

_____

_____

_____

• The blood cleanses me from:

_____

_____

_____

- I am forgiven through Jesus' blood for:

_____

_____

_____

- I come to the throne of God boldly because:

_____

_____

_____

- My inheritance in the blood is:

_____

_____

_____

- Because of Jesus' shed blood, I have fellowship with:

_____

_____

_____

- When I remember His body and blood in communion, I realize that:

_____

_____

_____

- Because Jesus shed His blood for me, I can:

_____

_____

_____

- I pray the covering of His blood over:

_____

_____

_____

What a joy it has been to share with you about the precious blood of Jesus Christ. What can we say? I say over and over again, "A million thanks, Jesus, for Your shed blood. A million thanks!"

My prayer for you is that you will apply the blood and walk in the authority and power of Jesus Christ each and every day. I pray His precious blood over you, dear saint. This is your day to experience and be cleansed anew though the blood in the mighty name of Jesus!

> *Thank You, precious Lord Jesus, for Your shed blood that covers and cleanses every one of us who are Your children. Amen!*

THE
LEADER'S
GUIDE

INTRODUCTION

THE LEADER'S GUIDE

The following pages contain a leader's guide for an introductory session and eight group sessions covering the weeks of this study guide. Each session will cover the studies the participants completed in the prior week.

Before the Introductory Session:

- Contact each group or class member, letting each know the time, date and location of your first group meeting or class.

- **Be certain you have the *The Blood* and *The Blood Study Guide*.**

- Order enough study guides for each individual in the group or class. Couples will find it difficult to share one guide as the exercises are focused for individual completion.

- You can order additional study guides from your local Christian bookstore or directly from:

  Charisma House
  600 Rinehart Road
  Lake Mary, FL 32746
  1-800-283-8494

- Have extra Bibles and pencils available in each group or class session.

- Use name tags for all group or class members for the first few sessions.

- Keep the group session time to about one hour. Respect the schedule of others. If it appears that the group needs more time for a particular session, reach a stopping time for those that must leave, end the session and then continue with those who wish to remain.

These study sessions are for:

- Individual believers studying about the blood.

- Small discipleship groups.

- Home groups.

- Prayer and Bible study groups.

- Sunday school classes.

- Men's and women's groups.

- Accountability groups.

Some things to remember about leading small groups are:

1. Encourage every member to participate. Do not let one or two people dominate the discussion or sharing times.

2. Contact group or class members who miss a session to encourage them to continue their studies and to be at the next session.

3. Before each session or class, ask the Holy Spirit to give you wisdom and discernment for the group and to guide the group process.

4. Pray regularly for all your group or class members.

5. Be certain that you have completed the studies for each week before you attempt to lead a group process.

6. Encourage all the group or class members to work through their study guides each week and to bring their study guides with them to the group sessions or classes.

7. Keep the group discussions and sharing times *moving*. Don't chase rabbit trails or become involved in arguments. Encourage, affirm and edify group members.

8. Find a person in the group who is willing to be your assistant to help with the group process and to lead the group in the rare event that you might have to miss a session.

9. Urge group or class members to be regular in their attendance. Missing a session should only happen if there is an emergency, illness or a trip out of town.

10. Promote or publicize your meeting. Invite people to attend starting with the Introductory Session. However, it would be very difficult for a new person to join this study after Session One.

11. Arrange for any child care if that is needed for a prospective group or class member.

It is our prayer that the Holy Spirit will guide and direct each session so that His presence will be felt and will become a transforming power in the lives of your participants as they study about the precious blood of Jesus Christ.

INTRODUCTORY SESSION

THE BLOOD

1. Welcome group or class members as they arrive. Give each person a name tag.

2. Give each person in the group a copy of *The Blood Study Guide*. Turn to Week One. Explain to the group the importance of each person committing to daily devotions for five days during each week, completing all the exercises in the study guide and reading the Scriptures. Tell the group members that each daily study will take about fifteen to twenty minutes.

3. Divide the group into pairs, grouping each member with someone not well known to each other. Give each person one minute to share a brief biography with his partner.

4. Have each pair find one other pair to form a group of four. Give the groups five minutes, instructing each person to introduce his or her partner to the other pair that has joined them in the group.

5. Bring the total group back together. Explain that in the weeks to come, some discussions and sharing times will be done by pairs, some in groups of four and some in the total group. Go over the Group Covenant at the end of this session plan with the group members. Invite group members to sign this page in their own study guides, indicating they will abide by the points in the covenant.

6. Go around the group, inviting each person to complete this sentence: *One thing I am excited about studying is*

_____

_____.

8. Ask for any prayer needs and then, as the group leader, close the group in prayer.

9. Tell everyone the time, location and date of the next group meeting or class.

A GROUP COVENANT

- Be on time.

- Be regular in attendance.

- Be willing to share openly and honestly.

- You will never be asked to share anything that would embarrass you or make you uncomfortable.

- Do not share outside of the group anything that has been shared in the group sessions. Remember to keep what is shared confidential.

- This is not a therapy group. Any personal problems that are shared can be prayed for, but further counseling must be sought outside the group process.

- Remember that this is a Christ-centered group that seeks to build up group members and the body of Christ through affirmation, acceptance, prayer, mutual respect and encouragement.

- If you agree with these points, sign on the line below:

_____

POWER AND PROMISE
IN THE BLOOD

1. Welcome each group member upon arrival, and see that everyone wears a name tag. Participants should have completed Week One in their study guides prior to this session.

2. With the total group, discuss: **How do you feel about the blood sacrificial system in the Old Testament?**

3. As a total group, discuss their answers to the Day 2 exercise on page 15: **On the lines below, describe a time when you may have tried to get God to do things your way. What were the results of your attempt?**

4. Divide the group into groups of four. Allow time for each group of four to discuss their individual answers to Day 3 exercises in the three areas of temptation as found on pages 18–19: **Check any temptation you are presently facing.** (Go over each list.)

5. Divide into pairs. Ask each partner to share the toughest temptations from the lists in Day 4 that satan puts before him or her. Encourage each person to share how the Lord gives him or her the power to resist.

6. In closing, invite the pairs to pray for one another so that they might resist temptation through the power of Jesus' blood. Suggest that they pray in particular about the temptations each individual mentioned in number 5 above.

SESSION TWO

THE BLOOD'S COVERING AND COVENANT

1. Greet group members warmly as they arrive. Be sure participants have completed Week Two in their study guides prior to this session.

2. Ask group members to share how they have been covering their families with the blood of Jesus during the previous week.

3. Invite those in the group who have a testimony about the protection of the blood's covering to share their testimonies.

4. Divide up into pairs or groups of four. Invite the small groups to discuss the principles they discovered as they completed Day 2 exercise on pages 33-34: **Read each scripture and then, on each line, write the reference that matches the principle.**

5. Invite the small groups to discuss their answers to Day 3 exercise on page 37: **Look over the following list. Circle anything that may be keeping you from becoming an obedient, living sacrifice to God. Describe any other hindrances you may have.**

6. Ask group members to share their responses to Day 5 exercise on pages 42-43: **To help you remember how He prospers you, read Psalm 103. Using that psalm as a basis, list the provisions mentioned in the psalm that you are experiencing in your life right now.**

7. In closing, form a circle and ask each person to pray for the person on their right, covering them with the blood of Jesus Christ.

APPLYING GOD'S
BELIEVER PROTECTION PLAN

1. Welcome group members warmly as they arrive. Participants should have completed Week Three in their study guides prior to this session.

2. Divide up into pairs or groups of four. Have these small groups share what they wrote in the doorposts on the Day 2 exercise on page 52. **Below is an illustration of a doorpost with the blood of Christ applied to it. Inside the door opening, write the names of family members whom you are now praying for and covering with the blood of Jesus.** Then as small groups, pray for those names written in the doorposts.

3. Reassemble the large group. Discuss some of the answers to Day 3 exercise on page 55: **Where do you need to apply the blood over your relationships and your possessions?**

4. Return to pairs. As partners, **share the last time you told someone else about the blood, spoke the Word to defeat the enemy or prayed and applied the blood of Christ to a person, place or situation.** (From Day 4 exercise on page 57.)

5. Encourage each partner to share the obstacles they are believing will be removed by faith through prayer.

6. In closing, have the partners pray for one another, moving mountains or seeking victory through the blood for one another.

SESSION FOUR

THERE'S CLEANSING IN THE BLOOD

1. Welcome warmly the group members as they arrive. Participants should have completed Week Four prior to this session.

2. On a chalkboard, overhead or flipchart, write this title: *The Work of the Holy Spirit.* **Ask group members to share the various ways the Holy Spirit works in their lives from what they discovered in the Scriptures** (from Day 2 exercise on pages 68–69).

3. As a group, discuss the various ways that people try to grow close to God. Then as a group, share how different members of the group have grown closer to God during the past week.

4. Divide into groups of four. Allow time for each group to share the responses to the Day 4 exercise on page 74: **Read each verse, and describe the blessings each verse gives for the believer who has access through Christ's blood and the indwelling Holy Spirit to the anointing of God.**

5. In closing, thank God for the atonement of the blood and the anointing of the Spirit on the life of each group member. Anoint each member of the group with oil as you pray.

SESSION FIVE

There's New Life in the Blood

1. Welcome warmly each group member as they arrive. Participants should have completed Week Five in their study guides prior to this session.

2. Allow several group members an opportunity to respond to this statement: **It's easier to forgive than to forget.**

3. Divide the group into pairs. Allow sufficient time for each partner to pray Psalm 51 over the other partner. Use Day 2 exercise on pages 85-86 for a guide: **Psalm 51 is an important psalm of confession and forgiveness. As you read the psalm, insert your name at each blank line.**

4. As a total group, compile a list of the benefits of redemption from the individual answers to Day 4 exercise on pages 90-91: **The Bible is filled with the benefits of what you have been redeemed to in your new life in Christ. Read each passage listed below and describe what you discover.**

5. Brainstorm the different ways they can share the good news of reconciliation with others. You may want to use some the individual responses to Day 5 exercise on page 94 for this list: **How are you sharing the message of reconciliation with others in the world?**

6. In closing, share the first names of people the group members know who need to be saved and who need to hear the Good News. As each name is shared, pray in unison, "Lord Jesus, we pray for the salvation of (name)."

JESUS, OUR MEDIATOR: GRACE IN HIS BLOOD

1. Greet the group members as they arrive, warmly welcoming them. Participants should have completed Week Six in their study guides prior to this session.

2. Share some of the feelings group members experience when they approach the throne of God in prayer. Use responses to Day 1 exercise on page 98: **When you approach the throne of God in prayer, how do you feel? With what attitude do you pray?**

3 Invite group members to share one thing they have interceded for most boldly in their prayer times. What happened when they prayed?

4. Discuss the following questions as a total group: **What pleases God about our prayers? What displeases God about our prayers at times?**

5. Invite group members who are comfortable in doing so to share some of the images of God they remember having as children.

6. On a chalkboard, overhead or flipchart, list some of the things that we have been set free from, and for, in our Christian lives. Use responses from Day 4 exercise on pages 108–109: **Read the following scriptures. Describe what each scripture says you have been set free from and what the scripture says you have been saved for.**

7. Invite the pairs to pray for one another, surrendering those things that need to be released into God's hands. As you close the session today, allow members to pray sentence prayers, thanking God for freedom through the blood.

SESSION SEVEN

GOD'S GRACE AND YOUR NEW FAMILY

1. Warmly welcome group members as they arrive. Participants should have completed Week Seven in their study guides prior to this session.

2. Divide into small groups. Discuss ways to show "Godlike" love to someone else. Use responses from Day 1 exercise on pages 117–118: **Beside each quality of God's love listed below, describe how you can show that love in a specific way to someone else.**

3. As a group, list the different aspects of our inheritance as believers from Day 3 exercise on pages 122–123. Have different group members share which part of the inheritance is most meaningful to them and why. **Scripture reveals many things about our eternal inheritance. Look up the following promises about your inheritance, and describe each one.**

4. In pairs, ask the group members to share how grace has empowered them to break the power of habitual sin in their lives or how they need the power of His grace to break a habitual sin. Use responses from Day 4 exercise on page 126 for this activity. **The Greek definition of *grace* includes both "free gift" and "joy." Complete the sentence, describing the effect of God's grace in your life.**

5. Reassemble as a group. Allow for a time of testimonies on how the shed blood of Jesus has been protecting, powerfully at work or cleansing individuals since the beginning of this study.

6. In closing, give thanks in prayer for the shed blood of Jesus.

SESSION EIGHT

COMMUNION IN
THE COMMUNION

1. Warmly greet the group members as they arrive. Group members should have completed Week Eight in their study guides prior to this session.

2. Ask everyone in the group to share one time of communion from the past that was very meaningful to them.

3. Share the Lord's supper together as a group. Be certain to bring the elements for the Lord's supper to this group meeting.

4. After communion, invite each group member to share one of the responses he or she made to the statements in the study guide for Day 5 of this week.

5. In closing, form a circle and ask each person to pray for the person on their right, covering them with the blood of Jesus. Close in prayer when everyone is done, praying God's protection and anointing upon each member as these sessions end. Thank each member for their participation, and encourage each person to live according to the principles they have discovered during this study.

Other Teaching Materials by Benny Hinn

The following books by
Benny Hinn are also available from
World Healing Center Church or from
your local Christian bookstore:

Good Morning, Holy Spirit
Welcome, Holy Spirit
The Biblical Road to Blessings
He Touched Me
The Miracle of Healing

World Healing Center Church
P.O. Box 162000
Irving, Texas 75016-2000